COMMUNICATION SECRETS
FOR SUCCESS

D1240155

n	f	l	x	i	f	w	z	h	n	n	l	x
j	i	i	a	o	i	y	e	t	o	v	i	a
h	j	i	n	f	j	x	w	n	m	x	i	n
i	k	f	a	m	i	l	y	h	o	q	f	a
q	k	t	u	n	k	o	w	n	u	y	t	u
i	b	x	n	o	b	v	u	l	e	k	x	n
l	n	r	c	a	r	e	e	r	o	c	r	y
p	y	l	y	m	n	e	l	i	y	a	l	c
a	c	d	a	u	c	a	q	h	g	r	d	a
s	b	k	z	e	j	n	o	t	i	e	k	z
z	z	j	e	o	o	c	k	x	v	e	j	e
h	z	a	w	y	y	u	o	r	y	r	a	w
k	c	p	q	g	c	n	a	l	w	m	p	q

BRIDGET SAMPSON

COMMUNICATION SECRETS FOR SUCCESS

By BRIDGET SAMPSON

Cover design by Kiran Robertson

Printed in the United States of America

First Printing, 2016

Best Living Books, Chatsworth CA 91311

www.BestLivingBooks.com

www.SampsonCommunicationConsulting.com

authorbridgetsampson@gmail.com

CONTENTS

INTRODUCTION

Do you remember that kid at school who had cooties when you were growing up? You know — the one everyone made fun of. The one nobody could touch without getting infected. I was that kid. No matter how hard I tried, I could not figure out how to make the other children like me. I desperately wanted friends but no one would take me on, for years. That period of my life ignited my fascination with communication and relationships. While I wouldn't relive it for all the money in the world, some of the benefits I derived are a keen sensitivity to how people are feeling and a tenacious desire to learn and teach others how to interact in ways that are uplifting, empowering, genuine, and egalitarian.

The quality of our relationships determines the quality of our lives. Satisfying, healthy connections are a result of conscious, compassionate communication. That's what this book is about... how to be a better communicator in all of your relationships. Some of my suggestions may not be relevant for you, but if you put into practice the ones that are, you can dramatically improve your life.

I wrote this book because I wanted to make the valuable information I've learned in academia and the business world accessible to a wider audience than my students and clients. I am compelled to translate complex theories and studies into everyday language and practical tips that can be readily applied in your daily life.

Who am I? I've been teaching communication studies courses (interpersonal communication, intercultural communication, organizational communication, beginning and advanced public speaking, etc.) at California State University, Northridge for twenty-five years. I'm passionate about my work and know that my students appreciate and gain a great deal from my dedication to preparing them for success — personally and professionally. I teach part-time, which means I'm not technically a professor. I'm what's known as a lecturer or adjunct faculty member. We're also often referred to as freeway flyers since many of us teach at multiple colleges and spend more time on the road than in the classroom.

I used to be a freeway flyer, but now I only teach two classes every Friday during the fifteen-week fall and spring semesters. I spend the rest of my professional time running a thriving communication consulting business. Most of my consulting work consists of creating and facilitating communication and leadership training programs for organizations. I also provide one-on-one coaching. My clients range from small nonprofits that advocate for foster youth, to large companies such as Google and Mattel. Though I have worked hard and remained steadfastly focused on my goals, I also feel truly blessed to get to travel the world doing what I love: helping people increase their communication competence to bring more joy and prosperity into their lives.

Now that you know my professional background, let's get personal. I've learned as much about communication from being a spouse, mother, daughter, friend, boss, employee, mentor, etc., as I have from all the textbooks and scholarly articles I've read over the years. That's why I decided to organize this book into conversational chapters on specific relationships and contexts in your life: communicating with your romantic partner or your boss, with an audience, and so on.

You can start anywhere. If your most troubling issues revolve around conflict with your children or children you care for, skip ahead to chapter four. If you struggle with negative thinking that weighs you down, start with chapter two, which is on communicating with yourself. Each chapter contains my top five tips on the subject along with one bonus fun tip. I spend more time on some tips than others, not necessarily because they are more important, but because I believe they need more explanation or elaboration.

I'll be referring to lessons learned from books, studies, research, and my personal life in a very non-academic manner and I make no apologies for that. I will shamelessly promote countless authors and teachers who I've learned from. You'll find a works cited and a recommended reading list at the end of the book, but I saw no need to take the time to formally cite all of my sources within each chapter. This is meant to be a practical guide for everyday living: an intimate conversation between you and me. That said, I encourage you to Google anything I mention, to explore it in greater depth or confirm its validity.

Here's a quick word about the difficulty level of the tips in this book. An early reader shared that while she enjoyed and agreed with most of my suggestions, a few of them would be tough to follow and she wondered why I didn't say much about that. I do realize that some of what I recommend may be challenging because of old habits, unhealthy patterns, fears and insecurities, etc. I also acknowledge that I didn't spend a lot of time mentioning all these potential difficulties. Let me tell you why: because I believe in your ability to change and become a better you. If you disagree with a suggestion and have a way that works for you while also being respectful and healthy for all involved, by all means, stick with it. But if you find yourself agreeing with what I say, yet repeatedly thinking, "But it's so hard to do that," please work to develop a more empowered mindset (chapter two covers this, by the way). If I can strive to do all the things I advocate in this book (even though, yes, they are hard sometimes), you can too. It may just require mustering up a little more confidence, patience, honesty, or restraint than you thought you had.

I don't want my suggestions to sound preachy or to imply that I think I've got it all figured out. I still make mistakes. I still occasionally dwell on how I could have said or handled things better. Understanding the profound impact that communication has on our relationships and working to make better choices is a lifelong journey, and I thank you for taking this one small step with me by reading my book. My greatest wish is that you find it helpful.

CHAPTER 1

COMMUNICATING WITH YOUR ROMANTIC PARTNER

1. DON'T SWEAT THE SMALL STUFF

Please forgive the cliché, but it fits perfectly here. After twenty-three years of marriage, many of the things that used to drive me crazy about my husband barely faze me now. I've realized I can live with dirty dishes in the sink, stinky socks on the floor, an unmet promise to fix a broken appliance in a timely manner, even an insensitive remark here and there. Thankfully, my husband has also learned to let it go when I break things, forget things, am still getting ready even though we're already half an hour late... wow, I'm realizing his list is probably longer than mine. The point is that all these minor infractions and more are forgivable and forgettable, if we choose to prioritize what really matters in a long-term romantic relationship. I'm not saying you should be so Zen that you have absolutely no internal reaction to these little annoyances. Inside, you may feel a twinge of irritation but that doesn't mean you have to act on it. Stopping to ask yourself whether there's really a need to say something before snapping at your partner with verbal criticism is a good idea.

I remember reading a study that analyzed the communication patterns in romantic relationships. One of the goals was to determine which factors were most common among those who stayed together and those who parted ways. I'll never forget reading that one of the greatest predictors of the eventual termination of a relationship was that the criticism to praise ratio was too high. So, frequent comments about disappointments over the little things without the balance of large doses of expressed appreciation and kindness may be the death knell for any couple.

I am well aware that not all relationships can or should be saved. But I worry that some relationships end because people realize too late that they were focused on the wrong things and didn't appreciate the good in their partners. A few days ago I was listening to a radio talk show about the recent increase in infidelity. I can't recall who the expert on the subject was, but he said something that resonated with me. He claimed that people often have affairs because they are looking for the 10% they feel their current partner is missing, while neglecting to appreciate the 90% that is wonderful and exactly what they want. The new lover may have that intoxicating 10% (attentiveness, romantic gestures, a strikingly attractive physical trait, or an interesting job to talk about, etc.). But what if the majority of his or her other 90% is all wrong for you? When you feel unhappy with your partner, take an honest look at the possibility that you need to change your own thinking instead of trying to change the other person.

The following is one of my favorite sayings, which sums up this recommendation well. It comes from Dr. Wayne Dyer, a favorite spiritual guru of mine. "When you change the way you look at things, the things you look at change." I believe this is as true for our romantic partners as it is for almost everything else in life.

2. TALK OPENLY ABOUT THE MOST IMPORTANT STUFF

Sex, finances, religion, needs, wants, expectations of fidelity, what hurts your feelings, what makes you feel loved and supported, what doesn't... we need to talk about it all. You have to find ways to engage in conversation about the tough subjects and to make your most significant needs clear.

I recommend the book *The Five Love Languages* by Gary Chapman. It was quite an eye-opener for my husband and me. Chapman explains that five love languages exist, one of which is primary for each individual. We naturally provide it and feel most loved when we receive it. The five love languages are: words of affirmation, quality time, receiving gifts, acts of service, and physical touch. If your primary love language is words of affirmation, you're likely to offer and appreciate frequent loving comments. If your love language is acts of service, you will want to run errands for your partner and take care of as many of his or her practical needs as you can. I'm sure you can see how many unnecessary hurts and disappointments could arise if you're not aware of your own love language and that of your partner. The good news is that we can learn all the love languages, enjoy them, and put them into practice with great skill. We aren't limited to the portion of the world that shares our primary love language. I also think there are probably way more than five love languages that we can discover through honest communication with our partners.

The first recommendation in this chapter is to hold your tongue more often when you're tempted to nitpick your partner to death with criticisms about his or her imperfections. Now I'm suggesting that with the big issues, you must talk about them openly, no matter how uncomfortable or fearful you may be about it. When you sweep important issues under the proverbial rug, they're almost certain to grow and multiply.

Discussing your deepest feelings and desires with your partner is essential, however, it does not guarantee a perfect long-term relationship. There will be disappointments and mistakes along the way. These can be overcome and forgiven if the two of you are willing to communicate openly about what went wrong and why. Both partners usually have some degree of culpability in these situations. Even with infidelity, when there appears to be one clear villain and one innocent victim, it's rarely that simple. While I don't recommend being unfaithful, I've seen a great many committed couples successfully work through it, especially if they seek counseling.

3. HAVE SEX OF SOME KIND, THAT YOU BOTH ENJOY, REGULARLY

Does anyone out there remember Dr. Ruth Westheimer? If you do, conjuring up her image is likely to put a smile on your face. If you don't, check her out online. I was thrilled to find that as I write this, she's still going strong at eighty-six years old. When I was growing up, she was a hugely popular sex therapist who you could regularly see on television or hear on the radio offering detailed sex advice for couples.

One of the most interesting things about Dr. Ruth was that she looked like someone's little old grandma, yet she was always talking about sex. I was only a child when I was first exposed to her and I'm so thankful for that because I remember thinking, "Wow, this sex thing must be really important for grown-ups, even this little old lady

8

is so into it." As an adult, even now that I'm hurtling toward becoming a little old lady myself, I believe more than ever that sex is very important. It's a basic human need along with food and shelter.

That's not to suggest that if you don't have a partner you should run out and recklessly fulfill your sexual desires with a stranger. The hormones released during sexual connection with another human being significantly increase the likelihood that you'll become emotionally attached to that person. Like it or not, we're hardwired so that when our bodies intertwine, our hearts, minds, and souls are pulled to come along for the ride. This is why I'm not a huge fan of the "friends-with-benefits" arrangement, though I know many people say it can work and I'd be open to hearing their arguments.

You may wonder what I mean by "regularly." That's a great question and there is no one-size-fits-all answer. I know couples that are very happy with once a week, especially those who have young children and are exhausted by all the demands on their time and energy. One woman I know who has been married for over twenty-five years and has three kids tells me that she and her husband do it once every evening and twice every morning. Kudos to them! Problems arise when there is a gap in the desired frequency of sex. So, yes, this is another issue that should be discussed. Tell your partner what you like, what you don't, and how often you'd prefer to be intimate. People are not mind readers.

When I say, "sex of some kind," I'm probably revealing my political beliefs more than anything else. I am an avid supporter of LGBTQ rights. In fact, I support the right of all consenting adults to do whatever they like with other consenting adults. I also know couples who, for religious or other reasons, chose to abstain from intercourse for some time. Yet, through honest communication and sometimes, even assistance from clergy, creative ways to share physical intimacy that fit with the couple's values were discovered. Again, the key is that partners must discuss and agree on what they want. Don't assume that what feels good to you feels good to your partner, whether you're the same or opposite sexes. I've heard way too many friends complain about having a partner do something unpleasant to them sexually but also report that they did not say anything about it. I must remind you again... as far as I'm aware at this point... WE CANNOT READ MINDS!

One of the best sex and relationship experts around today is Dr. Laura Berman. I've learned a tremendous amount from her. Check out her books and look for her television and radio shows if you want more great tips for healthy love relationships.

4. MEET 90% OF YOUR OWN NEEDS

One of the most helpful books my husband and I have read about relationships is *Why Mars and Venus Collide: Improving Relationships by Understanding How Men and Women Cope Differently with Stress* by John Gray. Gray is well known for his *Men Are from Mars, Women Are from Venus* books, a few of which I've also read. While I wouldn't want to overgeneralize the ways males and females interact in opposite-sex couples, many of Gray's observations ring true in my own relationship. Also, I would prefer to offer suggestions for couples that are applicable to same-sex marriages and long-term relationships rather than focus only on male-female coupling. But my favorite part of the book is definitely relevant in any romantic relationship.

Gray offers the metaphor of a fuel tank in a car, claiming that we should be able to fill our own tanks to about 90% and then a partner can provide that last 10% to top us off. What fills the tank? You have to answer that for yourself, but some possibilities are healthy self-esteem, great friendships and family connections, enjoyable work (paid or not), interests, activities, exercise, and a general contentment with life. Think about it. Wouldn't you want a partner who seems somewhat together and grounded with or without you?

We've all seen (and many of us have experienced) a partnership in which one person seems to need more than the other could possibly provide. I believe that when a partner is too needy — emotionally or otherwise — it's not likely that the relationship will be healthy and mutually beneficial. I think it would be worthwhile for each of us to consider what percentage of our tank we're able to fill on our own. Is it 90% for you? Or are you only at 40% or 50%? If your tank is low, it's time to work on filling it yourself because when you expect too much from a partner, he or she is likely to cave under the pressure of your unrealistic expectations.

5. COMMUNICATE WITH GREAT CARE AND SENSITIVITY

My parents' next milestone anniversary will mark half a century of marriage. I adore them and am in awe of their sweet, loving, affectionate relationship. I'm well aware that they are shining examples of putting my first four suggestions in this chapter into practice, yes, even number three. They've had ups and downs, of course, but never lost sight of what was important and fought hard to stay together. When I think about how my parents interact with each other, the words that come to mind are

11

easy-going, kind, generous, fun, positive, playful, and forgiving. While I've seen them argue and bicker at times, I've never seen them cross that clear nasty line we all know exists. They are careful in the way they speak to each other. Not so careful that you feel they hold back or censor themselves, but in a way that makes you feel that whatever they need to say to each other, they will do their best to say in a loving or gently teasing way. The most important thing to each of them is making the other feel loved, appreciated, and seen. Any little criticism or snide remark is always buffered with a laugh, a hug, or a kiss. There is just so much love and beautiful history between them that it's palpable for anyone in their presence.

Too often people in relationships don't think before they speak to one another, especially during a conflict. I'm guilty of this in my own marriage. It kills me to recall some of the hurtful and unnecessary things I've said to my husband over the years. And I can't take them back. What's worse is that when I'm thinking clearly, I can see that I didn't even actually mean most of them. When we are enraged, we are so much more prone to hyperbole, to making a mountain out of a speck of dirt. Anger floods the body with chemicals that trigger the fight or flight response. Flight is almost always a much better option. When we give in to the fight response, we say terrible, exaggerated, cruel things that we often regret later.

Emotional Intelligence by Daniel Goleman was a groundbreaking book released in the '90s. I remember the stir he created by suggesting that our emotional quotient (EQ) is as important as, if not more important than, our intellectual quotient (IQ). In the years since I read the book, what has stuck with me the most is a section called "The Anatomy of Rage." I learned a lot about myself from it. I may not have a perfect record of putting his lessons into practice, but they changed the way I deal with my anger in profound ways.

Goleman claims that those who demonstrate high EQ have the ability to circumvent the fight response when hostile feelings arise. They don't allow their rage to destroy their relationships. Goleman's findings show that there are two essential ways to do this: one involves a trait, the other a behavior. Let me warn you, these will not be anything you haven't heard before. But I hope you'll honestly ask yourself if you could make more of an effort to strengthen the trait and practice the behavior. I know I have room for improvement in both.

The trait is the ability to put yourself in the other person's place. When we are angry with another person, our tendency is to vilify that person and place most or all of the blame for the situation on him or her. We feel hurt or betrayed or slighted or whatever. The other person is bad and we are good. But in reality, if you give that person a chance to explain, there might actually be a perfectly understandable and maybe even forgivable reason for his or her words, actions, choices, etc. What can we do to build this muscle? Even in the heat of the moment, we can remind ourselves to calmly ask questions that start with something such as, "Can you help me understand what motivated you to…?" You may even get to the point of being big enough to admit that you might be mistaken: "What you just said kind of hurt my feelings, but maybe I'm taking it the wrong way. What do you really mean by that?"

The behavior that Goleman identified as being vital in moments of anger is the ability to walk away and allow a period of time to cool down before addressing the issue. This would mean consciously choosing flight over fight, at

13

least temporarily. The benefits of this option are numerous. If nothing else, all those hormones driving you to lash out at the other person in a fight will die down and you'll be able to more rationally consider how to communicate your needs and possible solutions. Taking a time out doesn't mean ignoring a problem: it means allowing time and space to consider how to logically and lovingly address it.

I believe that we can consciously choose to communicate with great care and sensitivity with anyone, anytime, even after a divorce or the dissolution of a relationship. Some people are not meant to be together romantically and decide it would be best to terminate that aspect of their connection. However, they often still need to co-parent, work together, share friends, or maintain other social ties. I also think we should choose to communicate this way even when the other person is not reciprocating. Gandhi's famous quote comes in handy here. "Be the change that you wish to see in the world." If we treat people the way we wish they'd treat us, we might be surprised by how much influence we truly have on others. Better still, we should strive to treat people the way we know they want to be treated, even if it's different from our own preferences.

6. BONUS FUN TIP: LAUGH TOGETHER

Many years ago I was having lunch with a trusted mentor who had been married for a very long time. She and her husband still seemed to enjoy each other's company after retiring from busy careers and welcoming grandchildren to the world. I asked her what she thought the secret to the success of her marriage was. I waited with anticipation as she contemplated the question while savoring a bite of spinach salad.

"We laugh a lot. We don't take things too seriously." It wasn't what I expected, but its simplicity and truth were undeniable.

I love to laugh with my husband. Nothing lightens and uplifts the mood in quite the same way. Sometimes we laugh about the silly things our kids do and say, sometimes my husband gets me started by doing this fake hearty laugh thing that somehow sparks a fit of hysterical giggling that I can't control. We love to watch live comedy shows or funny movies and television shows together. I'm sure you have your own ways to generate laughter and I recommend that you do it as often as possible.

I just did a little online research on the importance of laughing in romantic relationships and the science seems to support me here. One of the recommendations I found was to generate laughter through tickling. I sort of agree. There have been times a little playful tickling from my husband has been fun, but when he won't quit and my sides are aching, I really do want him to stop. So, tickle with care and stop when you're asked to, please!

The Bottom Line:

1. Let the little things go. We all have annoying habits. Be forgiving.
2. Talk about the important stuff: money, sex, needs, preferences, goals.
3. Make sure both partners' physical intimacy needs are being met.
4. Fill your own tank to 90%, so a partner can top off the last 10%.
5. Think, then speak. See his or her side. Cool down. Don't hit below the belt.
6. Laugh with your romantic partner and don't take things too seriously.

CHAPTER 2

COMMUNICATING WITH YOURSELF

1. BE AWARE THAT YOUR THOUGHTS CREATE YOUR REALITY TO A SIGNIFICANT EXTENT

I was recently listening to a talk by Christiane Northrup, a renowned doctor who specializes in women's health. I love the way she connects the dots between all aspects of our physical, emotional, and spiritual health. In this particular talk, Christiane reported that the average person has roughly 60,000 thoughts per day and about 87% of those thoughts are negative. Think about that. Could it be true for you? How might your life change if the opposite were true, if 87% of your thoughts were positive? A famous quote by Anne Lamott, another one of my favorite authors, makes this point with an interesting metaphor: "My mind is a bad neighborhood I try not to go into alone."

The never-ending conversation we have with ourselves in our own minds is often referred to as self-talk. Some say your self-talk is really your ego (the mean, nasty, judgmental critic) constantly trying to overpower your true self (the real you, who is brilliantly capable, gifted, and desperately wants to break free of the controlling, abusive ego).

When the movie *The Secret* was first released, I loved it and found it incredibly helpful in my life. It made perfect sense to me that what you constantly think about and tell yourself becomes your reality. I had learned about theories such as the law of expectations and the self-

17

fulfilling prophecy in legitimate university psychology classes and this new approach, dubbed "the law of attraction," seemed to be pretty much the same thing. I knew from personal experience that thoughts such as, "I'm so fat. I'll never lose weight," were sure to keep me overweight. Likewise, filling my mind with the idea that "I'm so broke, I can't seem to make enough money to get by," would only bring more of the same. This type of communication with the self has a powerful impact on what we believe we can do and the actions we choose as a result of those beliefs.

I was surprised when people began to criticize *The Secret*, suggesting that it's ridiculous to say that all you have to do is think about something to manifest it. It was as if people thought the makers of the film were saying that all you need to do is think about the new car you want and it will magically appear in your driveway. I don't think that's what they were saying at all. Of course you have to take action and usually have to work hard to achieve a goal. But if the conversation in your own mind is all about how you aren't really capable of doing it or aren't worthy of it, how could that not be creating a major roadblock? On the other hand, if your self-talk is positive and encouraging as well as forgiving when you slip, it seems reasonable to think that would propel you toward the finish line of your goal.

However, I say that your thoughts create your reality "to a significant" extent, and not entirely, for a very important reason. We don't all start the race at the same point. Some people are born with great advantages that set them up for success while others are born into such lack that reaching their full potential will be much less likely, though not impossible.

18

Oprah Winfrey and Barack Obama are not examples of what is probable, they are examples of what is possible if one overcomes great odds and obstacles. In the United States, roughly one in three black babies are born into poverty while only about one in ten white babies are. How can anyone argue that discrimination is dead and we now have a level playing field? It's ignorant and harmful to all of us to deny the damage done by slavery, the exploitation of low-paid workers, unequal wages and opportunities for women, etc. We have to own up to it and be honest about it. But, this does not mean that those who have more to overcome cannot achieve greatness.

Teaching and facilitating mentor training for the Educational Opportunity Program at California State University, Northridge has been one of the most rewarding experiences of my life. The program serves first-generation college students from historically low-income backgrounds. My heart breaks when I hear the stories of the unimaginable adversity some of these young people have faced. At the same time, I'm incredibly inspired by the fact that they never gave up on themselves and somehow found a way to attend college despite their circumstances. Though they may not realize it, many of them have become masters of the law of attraction by holding on to their belief that they can do and achieve more than anyone else in their families or communities ever dreamed was possible.

2. SPEAK TO YOURSELF AS YOU WOULD TO YOUR BEST FRIEND

The first point here is to develop an awareness of how powerful our thoughts are in shaping our reality. The next step is to control those thoughts and begin to battle the all-powerful ego bully with a kind, loving best friend. I can't say that I've figured out how to keep all or even most of my thoughts positive yet. I can only imagine how much better life would be if I could get my negative thoughts down to 30% or less. I do believe I'm moving in the right direction, however. Constantly nourishing myself with books, entertainment, and great discussions with like-minded people helps. But it's the enemy in my own mind that inflicts the most injury, so working to replace her with a kind, nurturing mentor is one of my biggest goals in life.

What works for me is to catch my negative thoughts as quickly as possible and replace them with more affirming self-talk. For example, I'm going back to teaching this week after a long winter break. I find myself worrying that my students won't like me, that I'll be boring, that I won't sleep the night before my first day of teaching, when I have to teach and hold office hours for eight hours straight with no real break. I'm sure you're familiar with this type of internal dialogue. It can be even worse when I have a big corporate gig. The imposter syndrome sometimes creeps up on me late at night in the hotel room, paid for by the client, along with the flight and my fee. My angry ego tells me that I have no business being there with all my expenses paid. I am only pretending to be a professional trainer teaching people how to communicate better and tomorrow will be the day I'm finally discovered.

Just writing these terrible, cruel, negative thoughts is making me uncomfortable. Why would I allow my ego to say these awful things to the real me? I would never speak to a friend or even a stranger this way! Would you? Of course not. So I must work to replace the thoughts. My worries about teaching can easily be swapped out for self-talk about how many years I've been teaching, the great evaluations I get from students, the wonderful support of my chair and colleagues, and how much I enjoy engaging with young people in the classroom. I can remind myself of similar successes I've had as a consultant and the many times participants in my training programs have thanked me for all that they learned in one of my sessions.

It's a bit embarrassing to admit this, but I keep a file of messages of appreciation from students and clients and I save nice cards from my family for those especially dark moments when I'm feeling down on myself. Thankfully, the majority of my ratemyprofessors.com reviews are positive so I can always go there too for a cheap self-esteem boost. (But please know that this is not a reliable source for students to judge professors — because for every student who posts a hateful critique, there are hundreds who loved that professor.) I'm sure you have similar resources that you can tap into when you need something to help you quickly replace those self-defeating internal messages with positive, healing, uplifting, empowering thoughts about yourself.

When you're feeling low, what kinds of things would your best friend say to try to make you feel better? You can just as easily have those same conversations with yourself in your own mind, if you choose to.

3. REPLACE THE LIES IN YOUR MIND WITH THE TRUTH

The mean voice in your head, your ego, not only says terrible things to you, it also lies to you all the time. So you have to be strong enough to let it know that you don't believe the lies and will not be dragged down by them.

Byron Katie wrote a book called *Loving What Is*. I'll never forget how it changed me when I read it. She suggests that when a thought pops into your mind that upsets you, you must immediately ask yourself if the thought is true. Let's say I look in the mirror and think, "I'm getting old. Our culture doesn't value old people so I'll be all washed up soon. No one will want to listen to what I have to say with all these wrinkles on my face." Is it true? No, it's not true. It doesn't have to be. I have the potential to live a full life for many more decades. At my age, I can be confident about all the experience and knowledge I've acquired, which causes people to respect me and take an interest in what I have to teach. I may have a few wrinkles, but they don't define me. They don't really matter at all — and that is what is true. Katie provides additional questions that will chip away at the might of your lying ego. Please check out her work.

Another set of lies we tell ourselves revolves around how unimportant we are, how boring our jobs and lives are, and how awful everything is. Replacing these thoughts with gratitude and new ways of defining ourselves and all the amazing things we do is a worthwhile exercise. In his outstanding ten-day audio program, "The Time of Your Life," Tony Robbins advocates coming up with fun, empowering titles for the roles you play in your life. He tells us, for example, that rather than just trying to be a romantic partner, you might think of yourself as a "sexual sensei." He coached a teacher who was feeling negative about having to be a "rule enforcer" to realize that she is actually a "developer of the human spirit." This may seem silly, but as you can probably tell, I love this kind of thing, so I was game.

Instead of thinking I'm just a teacher, I remind myself that I'm preparing future generations to solve the world's increasingly complex problems. Rather than feeling like a corporate trainer who's just teaching managers to manipulate people, I tell myself that I'm contributing to making the business world a more compassionate, innovative, and participatory environment. I'm not just a mom, I'm the caretaker of two unstoppable, brilliant young men who are destined to make all their dreams come true. Okay, I know this may all seem corny. If you're not willing to give it a try, at least promise me this... you'll never use the word "just" before any identity you claim for yourself.

4. BE GRATEFUL

For some reason, it seems popular to have a "life sucks and then you die" attitude these days. I'm not a fan of that standpoint. Your life is good — in so many more ways than it's bad. If you have this book in your possession, you have much to be grateful for. You probably have somewhere to live. You have food to eat. You have people who love you. You can read. Did you know that roughly 1/5 of the world's population is illiterate? You may have it harder than the next guy, but there's also someone who has it much harder than you.

Focus on what you have and it will grow. Focus on your lack and you'll get more of it. Be grateful for every little thing — every delicious meal, every kindness another person shows you, every day you're alive. If I could be guaranteed that you would follow-up on one of my recommendations, it would be this... I want you to watch the TED Talk, "The Happy Secret to Better Work" by Shawn Achor. He's not a self-help guru. He's a Harvard researcher. In this talk, Achor explains with crystal clarity how being happy and grateful will allow you to do everything in your life better. He helps us see that people have the success formula backwards. They think they'll be happy after they become successful. The research definitively disproves this. The reality is that when we are happy, grateful, and positive, we will be far more likely to be successful as a result.

Here's just a taste of what Achor's research shows: "Your brain in positive is 31% more productive than your brain in negative, neutral, or stressed. You're 37% better at sales. Doctors are 19% faster and more accurate at coming up with the correct diagnosis when positive instead of negative, neutral, or stressed. If you can find a way of being positive in the present, you will be better at whatever you're doing." If this grabs you, watch the video right away. It's likely you'll want more after that, so do what I did and read Achor's two phenomenal books: *The Happiness Advantage: The Seven Principles of Positive Psychology That Fuel Success and Performance at Work* and *Before Happiness: The 5 Hidden Keys to Achieving Success, Spreading Happiness, and Sustaining Positive Change.*

Two additional books that impacted my life in ways I could not possibly fully explain to you here are *The Power of Now* and *A New Earth*, both by Eckhart Tolle. While they taught me countless lessons about how to live a joyful and rewarding life, they also offered all the evidence you could ever ask for to prove that gratitude is an essential element for personal fulfillment.

5. USE MEDITATION FOR POSITIVE COMMUNICATION WITH YOURSELF

If my bringing up the idea of meditation makes you want to throw this book out the window, I get it. I have a love-hate relationship with meditation myself. I love it when I'm doing it regularly and I hate it when I'm not because I know I should be but I just don't want to, damn it! I'm currently in the "on" stage of this on-again-off-again love affair and deriving all the benefits (the pressure of writing a book and all the fears that come with it are great incentives). If you'll just read on, I can explain some of the astounding ways meditation can improve your life and a quick easy way to get started for just five to ten minutes a day.

Scientific studies show that meditation can boost your immune system, reduce stress, increase focus, and help fight depression, anxiety, addiction, ADHD, asthma, psoriasis, binge eating, smoking, and loneliness. Brain researchers found that regular meditators had thicker gray matter in the areas associated with self-awareness and compassion. Conversely, the areas associated with stress were smaller in meditators than non-meditators.

I've read about meditation and tried a variety of methods. I find that different approaches work for different people, so if you have one or know of one you can begin to learn that sounds right for you, go for it! For me, something called The Silva Method works well. My husband and I attended a weekend retreat to learn this simple yet powerful meditation practice and I applaud him for sticking with it much more consistently than I've been able to. I like the way it provides easy ways to bring yourself into a deeper state of mind and great phrases for positive message programming, such as, "Every day and in every way, I'm getting better and better." There's a whole lot more to The Silva Method and there are many other great programs out there.

As I mentioned earlier, even though I know all the benefits of meditation and have studied it extensively, I slip and fall into long periods of neglecting to do it. When I don't meditate, I am aware that I'm much more prone to negative thoughts and feelings throughout the day. So recently, I've decided to ease back in with my own method, which feels doable to start with and is based on different techniques.

I start by setting my phone timer for just five minutes. Ten is better if you think you can make it, but starting with five and building up to ten is certainly better than nothing. Focusing on the breath is almost always recommended in beginning meditation lessons. All you have to do is breathe deeply and focus on the breath in as it travels through your nose, into your chest, and fills your belly. Then slowly release the breath, focusing deeply on those same areas as it escapes them. Repeat. If you've ever tried to meditate, you're well aware of the concept of the "monkey mind." The ego will fight your attempt to clear the mind and will fill the space with a steady stream of thoughts, often negative or worrisome. The idea is not to resist the thoughts, but to let them pass and try not to get attached to them. They are just thoughts, not reality, and nothing you can or need to deal with at the moment.

We are supposed to dedicate a significant amount of our meditation time to get to a place of no-thought because when we can distance ourselves from our thoughts, especially those self-defeating ones, they have less power over us. I am trying to get better at this type of meditation. To be honest, I still have a hard time getting to the no-thought place. I use more of my meditation time to work on replacing negative thoughts, feelings, and messages with positive ones. This is why I consider meditation a form of communicating with myself.

As I breathe in, I tell myself what I'm breathing into my body and mind, as I breathe out, I tell myself what I'm breathing out. For example, while meditating, I might think to myself, "I'm breathing in confidence and power, I'm breathing out fear and weakness, I'm breathing in belief in myself and my abilities, I'm breathing out self-doubt." Sometimes I get specific, so today in my meditation before sitting down to write, I included, "I'm breathing out the fear that I'll never finish this book or no one will like it and breathing in the strength and confidence to just keep writing and trust the process."

The most recent book I read on meditation was *10% Happier* by Dan Harris. I loved it. You'll love it too. He is incredibly funny and irreverent and he was most definitely a skeptical, reluctant meditator at first. Following his journey from a high-stress, adrenaline-junkie TV news reporter to a true meditation teacher was pure pleasure for me. It motivated me to get back into it myself as well. Since I've been meditating daily for the past few months, I've gotten down to and maintained my ideal weight, exercise daily, am more relaxed with my husband and kids, have an abundance of extra energy, and have started several exciting projects in addition to my full-time work. This is just one of them! You really must try it!

Prayer can also be a powerful form of meditation — a way to communicate with yourself and your higher power, if you believe in one. Many people prefer to think of prayer and meditation as communication with their own higher selves. That can work too. Because I do believe in a higher power, though not one associated with a particular religion, conversation with that entity, which I see as a force of pure love in the universe, is very comforting for me. I attend a church that blesses and teaches from all spiritual texts and we meditate and pray during services, which leaves me feeling wonderful for the rest of the day. I have friends and loved ones who range from Atheists to devoutly religious. I would fully support whatever works for you and hope that it provides you with some practice that allows you to go deep inside, tap into something greater than yourself, and experience inner peace and a sense of connection to all that is.

6. BONUS FUN TIP: USE MUSIC AND DANCE TO COMMUNICATE WITH YOURSELF

Put on music that pulls you out of a bad mood and get up and dance to it. I personally love Zumba classes. Sometimes I'm overwhelmed by how great I feel when I get the choreography to a catchy song just right. If dance classes aren't your thing, I know music still is. We all have music we enjoy. Blast it in the car, in your living room, anywhere, and sing along until you feel your energy shift.

Song lyrics and tunes can remind us of beautiful experiences, dig up and release pain that we've kept buried, and break us out of feeling blah. Use the words and melodies that stir your emotions to communicate with yourself and help you feel whatever it is you most need to feel, whether it's a happy moment or a sad one.

Sometimes when I want to sink into feeling sad for a bit, I listen to the song "You Are The Sun" by Lionel Richie. This song takes me to a dark place quickly, because I listened to it over and over when my first boyfriend broke up with me. I thought my world had ended. He was everything to me — my sun. The song brings me back to a desperate, lonely place, which I actually need sometimes. In a way, it helps me release current feelings of sadness or loneliness. Then when it's over, and sometimes I will listen a few times just to steep in it, I feel better. I can see that I moved on from that time, just as I can move on from current and future heartache.

I always have a number of songs that can make me feel great instantly. They're usually contemporary pop songs but I know lots of people who find that classic oldies work better for them. Forgive me if these are out of date by the time you read this, but I want to provide a few examples in case you want to try them. "Brave" by Sara Bareilles makes me feel as if I can conquer the world. It's a brilliant confidence booster, especially if you sing along and dance. "Shake It Off" by Taylor Swift has a great message about not letting the criticism of others bring you down. If she can shake off all those haters who are so cruel to her, you and I can certainly deal with the difficult people in our lives, don't you think? "Uptown Funk" by Bruno Mars is probably my current favorite for making my spirit soar. I don't even know why. I don't even understand some of the lyrics, but still it has a magical effect on me, so I listen to it regularly. You have a song like that, don't you? If you don't, I suggest you find one immediately!

The Bottom Line:

1. Work to replace your negative thoughts with a more positive perspective.
2. Speak to yourself with kindness. Stop letting your ego bully you.
3. Don't believe the lies your mind tells you. Seek your own inner truth.
4. Remind yourself of all that you're grateful for regularly.
5. Meditate to experience more calm, joy, ease, balance, and abundance.
6. Allow music to help you feel what you need to feel.

CHAPTER 3

COMMUNICATING WITH YOUR BOSS

1. SEE AND TREAT YOUR BOSS AS A HUMAN BEING

In my role as a trainer and consultant in a variety of organizations over the years, one of the things I've found most perplexing is people's harsh judgment of their bosses. As an external advisor, who's not officially a member of the organization, I seem to make entry level and middle management employees feel comfortable enough to unload their enormous knapsacks of complaints about their leaders. What these individuals often don't expect is my response, which is usually an attempt to get them to understand things from their boss's point of view.

The types of comments I typically hear from people in leadership positions are: "I try my best to make things easier on my staff but they don't seem to notice or appreciate anything I do," "I know this is difficult for them, but I feel like they don't understand the big picture, even though I've shared it with them many times," and, "I'm aware that they feel overwhelmed by their daily tasks, but I don't think they realize how overwhelmed I am too, and how much is at stake. I'm trying to keep our department afloat." I believe that most leaders are truly doing their best to meet all the demands of the business they're in as well as those of the staff they manage. Many leaders I've come across have no training in how to manage people. They tend to be high achievers in their field and so they're thrust into a management position that forces them to produce at a much higher level individually and to now figure out how to inspire, motivate, educate, mentor, and move a group of other people to produce impressive results as well. It's a tough spot to be in, and I find that too many people who've never been in it have little compassion or empathy for those who are struggling to do it well.

You can find many statistics to prove that the burden placed on managers today is like nothing we've seen in the past. Keep in mind that they are actually human beings as well, with families, friends, hobbies, and a desire to do the right thing. I will admit that with so many pressures and high expectations weighing them down, people in high-level positions may at times forget to practice their best communication skills. Your boss may snap at you for making a mistake. She shouldn't. Your boss may not clearly explain the instructions for your new project. He should. I understand all this and I've been there, but taking these things personally and getting upset about them won't help you. Trying to see your boss as a human being who faces great pressures, many of which you're not even aware of, will help you. Stay calm. Ask for clarification. Ask how you can help. Do your best. I've found that regardless of how gruff or unsupportive some bosses may seem, they will almost always offer mentoring and unwavering loyalty to those employees who work hard, meet their commitments on time, and are willing to learn and grow.

2. ACCEPT AND APPRECIATE CONSTRUCTIVE CRITICISM

The first time I taught a leadership course in the corporate world, well over a decade ago, for a Fortune 500 company that was the most successful in its industry,

I was pretty nervous. I had minimal experience managing people myself, other than a few interns, assistants, and part-time employees. I had to keep reminding myself that despite all this, I did know how to teach. I had been teaching communication courses at a university for many years, so I could and would figure out how to teach leadership to "real" leaders. I diligently studied the facilitator guides I was given to prepare to teach this monster of a six-day course covering topics from managing change and conflict resolution to setting goals and delivering performance reviews. As I moved through the material, I remember how surprised I was by one of the statements I read about how managers feel about providing feedback for improvement. While I knew that I personally dreaded it and avoided it at all costs, I had never fully realized the extent to which most people feel exactly the same way. The facilitator guide actually listed avoidance as the most common tactic leaders take when they need to tell an employee that some type of improvement is needed.

While this intuitively made sense to me, it didn't jive with the common refrain I regularly heard from non-management employees that all their bosses ever do is criticize them. How could so many people feel that they were constantly being coached to improve when that was the very kind of coaching leaders were most likely to steer clear of? I haven't exactly figured out the answer to that question, but I know it's somehow connected to the huge gap between perception and reality that we all live with and need to work harder to bridge.

The truth is, contrary to what you might believe, telling you that you aren't doing as well as you could be in some aspect of your job is likely a very, very difficult thing for your boss to do. No matter how badly he or she botches the conversation and presents it with minimal tact (often out of fear of your denial and defensiveness), it was almost certainly as unpleasant for the giver as it was for the receiver. If you can, imagine that the roles were reversed and you had to tell someone something that they didn't want to hear and that might ruin their day, week, or year. No fun at all, right?

I once had an interesting conversation with a colleague about this very issue. He had an unusual take on the subject that inspired a bit of a paradigm shift for me. The first thing he said was that we should always immediately express gratitude for any kind of performance feedback. Then he explained that if your boss criticizes you in some way, you should quickly assess your feelings about it and choose one of three options. The first feeling might be complete denial. You believe the accusation is untrue, unfair, or is some kind of misunderstanding. In this case, your response should be something along the lines of, "I appreciate that feedback. Can I think about it and get back to you to discuss the issue further?" Taking time to think about it can provide you with time to construct a clear, non-defensive explanation that might shed new light on the subject for your boss. Or it might lessen your defensiveness and force you to see that there's some truth to the criticism, in which case you can move to the next option.

In the second potential situation, you can admit that there is some truth to the feedback, but you feel there is more to the situation and you'd like a chance to explain. It's still not a good choice to respond defensively. One of my favorite sayings about this kind of scenario is that explanations are welcome, while excuses are not. A statement similar to the one I recommended in the first type of situation works here as well. But you could also add something such as, "Can we make some time to talk about it tomorrow? I realize I could have done better and I don't want to make excuses, but I think there were some complicated factors involved that I'd like to get your take on. That way I can avoid the problem in the future."

In the third case, you're a big enough person to be honest and just admit that you messed up. We all do from time to time. What you want to do is admit it right away without letting the denial monster waste everyone's time and energy. You didn't do what you should have or didn't do it in a timely manner. You simply dropped the ball this time. Admitting it does not lessen your power or credibility, it increases it! Because believe me, your boss is well aware of the truth. This response is a no brainer. You fess up, take responsibility, accept accountability. The easier you make this on your boss, the more he or she will love you. Just say, "Yeah, you're absolutely right. I should have/I shouldn't have... and next time I'll make sure to..."

3. DEMONSTRATE THAT YOU RESPECT YOUR BOSS'S TIME

One of the things I love about one-on-one communication coaching, as opposed to large-group training, is that we can dig so much deeper into individual challenges and obstacles to success. I was working with a mid-level manager recently who had been told that his company would be investing in communication coaching to hone his professional communication skills as a gift to him. While I do believe coaching is beneficial, those on the receiving end of having it mandated by their employer rarely have such a positive view of it, at least initially.

Let's call the employee I was coaching Carl and say his boss's name was Melinda. Melinda confided in me that Carl's presentations were way too long and that he talked about his personal life at length, even with senior executives. While his speeches were dynamic and engaging, and he was affable and relaxed interpersonally, his awareness of the appropriate length of time to give a report, tell a story, or share a personal anecdote was sorely lacking. When I pressed Melinda on the issue of how she herself had broached the subject with Carl, it became clear that she couldn't bring herself to do it, even in the most indirect manner. So these are the fun kinds of missions that are passed on to consultants like me.

In sessions with Carl, I had him deliver sample reports and was able to coach him on how to make his points more clearly and concisely, which he seemed to appreciate. I mean who doesn't want more time in the day? As we worked on one of his weekly updates, we were able to condense what originally took him fifteen minutes to deliver down to about eight and a half. I used this opportunity to praise him (the number one motivating factor for most employees, according to numerous studies, by the way) for his understanding of how important it is for professional communication to be as brief as possible. He agreed that most people in his organization were so busy (which is true for every organization I've ever worked with) that there was no time to waste on superfluous information. I reminded him that this is especially the case with senior executives. I joked that if I only had a nickel for every senior executive I'd heard lament, "Why can't she just give me the bullet points?" or, "Why can't he just get to the bottom line?" I'd be sipping a fruity cocktail on a beach in the Caribbean instead of being in a conference room with him.

All this led to the hard part, which was having to point out to Carl that at the beginning of our session, I was actually timing him as he made small talk about his personal life. He appeared shocked and embarrassed to learn that he talked about his wife's broken foot, his kids' sports and activities, his dogs, his recent ski trip, and home improvement projects for over twenty minutes of our two-hour session. Yes, I felt like a complete heel for having to do this, but I kept telling myself it was for his own good. I had to dig the knife in deeper by asking him if it was possible that he gets equally carried away and loses track of time this way when chatting with his boss and other senior executives. The shame of his apparent realization that this was probably the real reason behind why I was brought in showed on his face and I seriously wanted to hug him. But I've been through too many sexual harassment training sessions to make that mistake.

This story is intended to make two main points. Though I love my coaching work, I don't want you to get to the point of needing to be coached by an outside party. Ask for feedback for improvement from your leaders, make noticeable changes, and repeat... over and over. Look at your communication honestly and work to get better at it, always. We never get to perfect in this area, no matter how much we practice. None of us. The second point is to keep your communication as concise as possible to show that you respect the valuable time of the busy people you work with, especially those senior to you. I'm definitely in favor of making personal connections, sharing tidbits about our lives outside of work, and showing that we're interested in one another as people as well as co-workers. But this kind of sharing should not take up large chunks of time during working hours.

I just finished the book *Influencing Up* and I highly recommend it for those of you who would like to have more sway with those who are senior to you in your organization. It's chock-full of great tips. Some of the most important are that if you want to be more influential with senior leaders, you need to understand their goals, contribute to achieving them, and do your best not to add to their work or concerns. These are excellent ways to build your professional power and to show your boss and other higher-ups that you respect their time.

4. TOOT YOUR OWN HORN, BUT DO IT SPARINGLY AND STRATEGICALLY

Most bosses are too busy to micromanage their employees, which is a good thing because it's important for people to be autonomous and to have room to experiment and learn on their own. However, because leaders are often spread so thin, they're not always aware of the great work members of their team are doing. I'm sure you're familiar with what can happen as a result. Just as the squeaky wheel gets oiled, unfortunately the biggest bragger usually gets more recognition and rewards than those who toil away with too much humility to bring attention to even their most stellar contributions.

Learn to share your accomplishments with your boss from time to time. Keep track of any form of positive feedback you receive. If you get a glowing email message from a customer, keep it in a file with others. You might want to select one of the best ones to forward to your boss with a brief FYI message. If a senior executive praises the clarity of the data on your PowerPoint slides when your boss isn't present, find a way to share how honored you were to receive this feedback from someone you look up to in the organization. When you go above and beyond expectations in your work, such as staying in the office until midnight to meet a near-impossible deadline or conducting extensive research to help the team make a well-informed decision on an important issue, don't complain about it. Sorry to be blunt, but no one wants to show appreciation to a whiner. Say something like this instead, "It took a lot of extra work to dig up and make sense of all the statistics on the marketing campaign options, but I'm so glad I did because the sales figures clearly show that we made the best choice."

If you choose to try this tip, please do so with great caution. There is a fine line between appropriately pointing out when you've done something valuable and boasting. Tooting your horn sparingly means that you mention your accomplishments on occasion, not daily. Being strategic means that you select your highest value contributions, those that demonstrate that you far exceeded expectations. It's important to be strategic about the time and place as well as the content of your message. When your boss is in a hurry, stressed-out, or caught up in a difficult situation, it's clearly not the best time to ask for a pat on the back.

5. BUILD A PERSONAL RELATIONSHIP WITH YOUR BOSS

Before you can do this, you must earn your boss's respect by being a high performer, meeting deadlines, and being dedicated to your work. If you're not entirely certain that you're excelling in all these areas, set this book aside and read one of the many guides out there on how to be more successful. One of my all-time favorites is *The Success Principles* by Jack Canfield. When my husband recommended it to me, he made the bold claim that even if I only applied the first of his sixty-two success principles to my life, I would see dramatic results. He was right.

If your performance and your attitude are both positive and consistent, it's likely that your boss would be open to building a more personal, friendly relationship with you. Share your interests and passions — those relevant to your field as well as those outside of work. Be careful to pay attention to verbal and nonverbal cues about what subjects your boss is comfortable discussing though. If you get dead silence in response to a personal disclosure, you probably went too far and will want to change the subject quickly. Show genuine curiosity about all aspects of your boss's life to find out how you can better connect with him or her. When you get to know someone on a more intimate level, working together can be much easier and less stressful.

My husband owns a small business with seven employees. He enjoys getting to know them and hearing about what their kids are doing or about a new pet or interest outside of work. I admire the way he cultivates relaxed, friendly relationships with his employees. I also know that it means a lot to him when they open up to him and trust him with information about their personal lives. It's a gift that they give to him. So give your boss a chance and take the risk of connecting on a deeper level than you have in the past. But please, please, do not forget my admonishment in number three above! If it works for both of you, it's great to be able to spend time away from work sharing a meal, a happy hour, a concert, exercising, or doing some other enjoyable activity to build your relationship in this way, rather than trying to squeeze it into a hectic workday.

6. BONUS FUN TIP: HELP YOUR BOSS HAVE FUN AT WORK

I just read an online article titled, "10 Ways to Make Your Boss Laugh." There were some good suggestions, the first of which is to figure out your boss's sense of humor. Once you've done this, you can periodically email a silly cartoon you know he or she would appreciate or tell a quick joke you read on the Internet to kick off an update meeting.

If you've made the effort to build a personal relationship, chances are you have a good sense of what your boss enjoys. Would incorporating a game or icebreaker into a team-building session you've been asked to lead help him or her loosen up and have a little fun? Would planning a bowling outing or softball game for the team allow your boss to show off some hard-won skills?

Get to know your boss, appreciate that being a leader is an incredibly tough job, and do what you can to lighten the load and help him or her find more joy at work.

The Bottom Line:

1. Have compassion for your boss. Seek the good in your boss and you'll find it.
2. View constructive criticism as a gift that helps you become a better you.
3. Don't ever waste or take up too much of your boss's time.
4. Tout your big accomplishments occasionally to get the credit you deserve.
5. If you produce outstanding and timely results, get friendly with your boss.
6. Figure out what your boss considers fun and make it happen!

CHAPTER 4

COMMUNICATING WITH CHILDREN

1. LISTEN TO THEM

Attending my younger son's first debate tournament, when he was thirteen, was an incredible learning experience for me. These kids had so much to say. They had powerful arguments and eloquently articulated the research they had done and opinions they had formed. It occurred to me that they must relish this opportunity to speak at length about all the things they think and know without being interrupted or treated as if they don't have much to contribute to a conversation because of their age. I watched with fascination as this tiny little seventh grade girl asserted her claims with great force and thought about how I would never have expected such brilliant words to come out of her mouth, and with so much poise and confidence! If we give children and teenagers the opportunity to speak their minds more often, they will surprise us with all that they have to say.

Most young kids love to talk and are too frequently shushed or cut off because we assume that what they have to say isn't important. It is. I often notice adults ignoring the kids in their presence as they chat about adult topics. Then if a child tries to join in, a parent may angrily bark something such as, "Don't interrupt Mommy when she's talking to Aunt Martha!" This makes me so sad. Why should that child not be included in the conversation? Why are the same things we do (change topics, interrupt one another, add a thought to a discussion) considered rude when a child does them? I

UNITED TSA Pre✓

SCHIFFER/OLIVIAELIZABE

UA-****594

Los Angeles to Newark Liberty Intl

UA1729

LAX - EWR 75D

WED 03 AUG 2016

Gate May Change

GATE	BOARDING BEGINS	SEAT

1 : 25 PM

Boarding Ends: 2:00 PM Aisle
Board Departs: 2:15 PM Economy
Flight Arrives: 10:40 PM

37D

BOARDING GROUP

5

Confirmation: **MD6R6N**

MD6R6N 37D 95
UA1729 ELAX000_

The United MileagePlus® Explorer Card.

- Free checked bag[1]
- Priority boarding privileges
- Two United Club℠ passes
- Double miles on United® tickets
- Use miles to book any seat, any time

MileagePlus Explorer
UNITED | CHASE
VISA Signature
D. BARRETT

For additional details and to apply, go to UnitedExplorerCard.com.

1 FREE CHECKED BAG: Free bag is for first standard checked bag for the primary Cardmember and one companion traveling on the same reservation. Service charges for additional/oversized/overweight bags may apply. Purchase of ticket(s) with Card is required. See www.united.com/chasebag for details.

Terms and limitations apply. United MileagePlus credit cards are issued by Chase Bank USA, N.A. Offer subject to change.

7/15

...mergency Contact - Name/Relationship | Area Code or City & Country Code & Phone

...st Name(s)/Surname(s) | Middle | First
...ional)

...EQUIRED)

For applicability, please ask the United Representative.

...traveling on international flights. Please complete the following.

...egulations, airlines are required to obtain the full name of customers

...o comply with U.S. Department of Transportation and other country

think we often exclude children from our conversations in ways we wouldn't consider acceptable to do to adults. If you give them a chance, even young children might actually be able to contribute and learn more from being included than you can possibly imagine.

Ask children questions. Listen to their answers with interest and then ask more questions. Ask open-ended questions. Ask kid-friendly questions. When my kids were young, I discovered pretty quickly that, "How was school today?" was guaranteed to be met with, "Fine." No elaboration. So I tried out a number of alternatives. Many failed. One that seemed to work well with my boys turned out to be, "Did anyone get in trouble at school today?" I got lots of juicy stories and insights about what was going on with that question!

As my own kids have gotten older, I've been blessed with the opportunity to babysit my younger niece and nephews almost every Sunday for about six years now. What fun it is to ask them all kinds of questions that allow them to reteach me some of the things I forgot from my early years in school. On top of that, I get the added benefit of seeing the world through their glorious rose-colored glasses for a while.

Now that my sons are teens, I ask a lot about who's dating who, which teachers annoy them and why, what school rules drive them crazy, etc. I try to ask questions they'd want to answer, not questions I would ask someone my own age. Then I do my best to set aside the many distractions (my smartphone, the emails I need to answer, the book I'm trying to write... we all have endless excuses) and truly, deeply, actively listen to what they have to say.

One last word on listening... we have to listen to babies too. They may not have words but their cries send a clear message that they need something. It may be food, physical touch, a diaper change. When you are tuned in to a baby, you can usually tell which cry it is and meet that child's need. If you really can't figure it out, holding a baby close, rocking and singing or speaking softly almost always does the trick. I know there are parenting philosophies that will tell you it's okay to let a baby cry it out alone for an hour or more. I don't believe in them and the psychologists and pediatricians who have earned my respect don't either. When our babies cried, and one of them cried all the time, we figured out what they wanted and did our best to meet that need so that they would feel loved and secure in the world.

2. USE CONVERSATIONS AND CONSEQUENCES RATHER THAN FORCE

I know this may be controversial, but I have to say it. I have read a lot about spanking and based on what I've learned, I don't believe it's an effective form of discipline. The research I've found suggests that children who are spanked may have lower IQs, be more prone to violence, and have lower critical thinking skills than kids who are never spanked. This all makes sense to me because spanking is a convenient way to correct a behavior in the moment, but it does not encourage critical thinking about choices and consequences. Children do as we do, not as we say. When you spank a child, you send the message that hitting someone is a good way to respond to a behavior you don't like. Is that really what we want to teach our children to do? How can we tell them not to hit others if we're hitting them? I can't imagine the confusion that must cause. I believe that natural consequences and lengthy discussions about making good choices are

45

much more humane and effective ways to teach our children right from wrong.

We made the choice early on as parents never to hit or use physical force to discipline our children. It has been difficult to stick to that commitment, but we have. I completely understand the desire and have felt it countless times. Many friends and family members who I adore spank their kids. My mother spanked me a few times and I think she's the most wonderful mother who ever lived, so I'm not judging here. I know you love and would do anything for your kids. It's really about what works and what we're teaching our children. My sons will tell you they would have rather had a quick spanking than have to listen to our long lectures about why we have certain rules and expectations, how to make better choices, and why we've chosen to take away a particular privilege as a consequence.

One of the basic tenets of human psychology is that positive reinforcement works far better than negative reinforcement. If you want to use the most effective means of encouraging children to repeat desired behaviors, reward them. Just as giving our dogs a treat when they follow commands is the best way to get them to learn a new trick, our kids are conditioned to excel and make good decisions when they get plenty of recognition and praise from adults for doing so.

3. MINIMIZE YELLING AT THEM

Do you yell at your co-workers when they frustrate you? (I'm trusting that the answer is a horrified no here.) Do you yell at your friends when they've let you down? (Same expectation.) Would you yell at the cashier at the store when she accidentally gives you the wrong change? My assumption is that if you've picked up this book, you are already a conscious communicator and would consider yelling at someone in any of the above situations in terribly poor taste. So, then I would ask you, why would you yell at children when part of their learning process is to make mistakes, break rules, test boundaries, and do things that don't make any sense to us? They must do these things to learn the lessons they need to learn. A baby in her high chair who keeps intentionally dropping things on the floor is not trying to create extra work for you, she's working to grasp the complex concept of gravity. When you look at it that way, doesn't yelling at her in response seem cruel? Not only that, you'd be circumventing her learning process by discouraging scientific experimentation.

I have yelled at my kids. My record is not perfect here. But I usually feel terrible afterward. I also usually realize that if I had calmed myself down and thought about the best way to respond, there would have been a better alternative. When my kids were young and I yelled at them, it often led them to cry and be so upset that they couldn't actually focus on listening to what made me so mad and why. Doesn't that defeat the purpose of trying to teach children what they did wrong? When I hear people yelling at their kids, I often cringe because as an outsider, I can see that it's not the best choice. It's tougher to see that when it's our own kids or even the kids we're babysitting or have spent a lot of time with. When you want to yell at a child, stop and slowly count to three, then think about what it is you want to teach the child and do it calmly, with age-appropriate reasons provided. Imagine that you're a kindergarten teacher. You wouldn't yell at the children in your class all day long. You'd have to repeatedly make your expectations known and then calmly point out every time an expectation was not met.

Yelling is a form of verbal abuse, maybe in your opinion it's a mild one, but in my opinion it is a harmful and unnecessary one. There is always a way to firmly make your point without yelling it. If we can figure out how to do it at the office with the co-worker who seems to get everything wrong, we can certainly do it with the children in our lives who we want to feel empowered, encouraged, and safe.

I know there are exceptions to this rule. For example, if your child is about to step into the street in front of a bus, by all means... scream your head off to stop him or her.

4. DON'T FIGHT IN FRONT OF THEM: TABLE THE DISCUSSION UNTIL YOU CAN BE ALONE

A long time ago, on an episode of the Oprah show, Oprah and Dr. Phil discussed the issue of parents fighting in front of their kids. As a viewer, I shared Oprah's "aha moment" when Dr. Phil said, "When you fight with each other in front of your children, you forever change who they are." Just the thought of the insensitivity, unkindness, and harsh judgment that so many of us have modeled for kids by fighting with other adults in front of them breaks my heart. I have been guilty of this. My kids have seen my husband and me fight. I would take those times back if I could, but I can't, so all I can do is be sure not to do it anymore.

We don't fight in front of our children. We do our best to model loving kindness, forgiveness, and a willingness to let the small things go and cherish our relationship. When a conversation with another adult becomes heated and children are present, please do the mature, responsible thing and table the discussion until you can continue it alone. I believe the world would be a very different place if people made this simple choice.

My older son is an adult now, so I have many new opportunities to see what he has learned from us — good and bad. He has had a wonderful girlfriend for a long time and while I try to let them have their privacy, I hear and see things when they're at our house. It's comforting to realize that he has inherited my husband's calm emotional demeanor. My son is very open with his feelings and I now feel that I can talk to/ask him about pretty much anything. Like my husband, he's not quick to anger. If there's a conflict or issue, he looks at it rationally. I don't hear him having nasty fights with his girlfriend or friends. I hear him trying to analyze situations logically and offer solutions. I hear him apologizing when he falls short of someone else's expectations.

While we may have made the mistake of fighting in front of our children a few times early on, the saving grace is that the love, kindness, and respectful teamwork my husband and I work hard to consistently demonstrate in our home appears to have played a bigger role in shaping the people they are becoming. Perfect parenting doesn't exist, but please do your best to model compassion, forgiveness, understanding, and willingness to compromise during conflicts rather than fighting.

My views on mindful parenting have recently been transformed by the work of Dr. Shefali Tsabary. I highly recommend her book, *The Conscious Parent*, and her TED talk of the same name. I have studied many parenting philosophies over the years, but Dr. Tsabary's powerful lessons shed new light on the many ways that we unknowingly harm our children and how we can begin to do better.

5. RESPOND TO THAT REBELLIOUS TEENAGER WITH COMPASSION

I'm in the thick of the teen years with my kids and it has almost killed me. And I thought the sleepless nights of having an infant were tough! Piece of cake! Okay, I'm exaggerating a little. But, wow, these years have been much more difficult than I ever imagined, despite all the warnings from parents who've been there. I have to share something here that I hope my kids will forgive me for revealing. They've both experienced therapy and we've all also attended family sessions with their therapist, who specializes in teens, and I've learned a tremendous amount about how to parent teens (male teens in particular) from him. On top of that, the therapist has some kind of magical powers that cause my kids to open up to him about the kinds of things teens do not want to talk to their parents about. I'm incredibly grateful for the help he has provided for our family. So, if you are the parent of or know a teen who seems to be struggling a lot, I would recommend counseling. It may seem costly, but many communities have programs that offer therapy on a sliding scale that goes down to almost nothing and in some cases can be free. My insurance through my employer reimburses us for a significant portion, so please look into that as well.

The main job of a teenager is to differentiate from his or her parents to move toward becoming a self-sufficient, autonomous adult. This explains why a teenager will disagree with something you say even if what you've said makes perfect sense or is an indisputable fact. It can be incredibly annoying, infuriating at times, but it's also perfectly normal and a sign that a teen is on track developmentally. Responding with frustration or over-explaining your own point of view on every issue a teenager disagrees with you on may literally drive you mad. Please believe me, I know because that was my default tactic when I first entered this frightening world. When I learned that I didn't have to do that (I wish it would have been sooner) life became much more bearable.

The phrase "choose your battles" may sound simplistic, but if you live with, work with, or in any way interact with teenagers, it is sound advice that you'll need to follow on a daily basis — if you want to retain your sanity.

If you're not at this stage yet and will be at some point, let me prepare you with brutal honesty: teens/young adults will likely do things that scare the life out of you and/or enrage you, especially if you are their parent. They will often break even your most firm rules and stomp on the most cherished values you've worked so hard to instill in them for their entire lives. I'm sorry, but this just seems to be part of the journey of parenting — one of the most crushing parts. Please know that when they hit this stage, it is almost always temporary. We went through it early, when our older son was only fourteen. It was hell. Years later, we're all on the other side and he's one of my favorite people again. I adore him. I shudder to imagine what you would have thought of my feelings about him when we were in that hell. I know other parents whose kids were perfect angels their entire lives and then completely lost it in the final year of college — doing drugs, failing classes, being belligerent and hateful toward the very parents who had funded their education and given them everything. Whenever it happens, it's awful, the worst. But again... it is almost always temporary. They do come back around.

This kind of situation is all but guaranteed during the teen years. I know some parents get lucky and don't go through it, or just aren't aware of what their teens are doing when they're not around, but from what I've seen it happens more often than not. This may sound strange, but no matter how bad things get, it's critical that you love and accept the teenager/young adult through it all. Consider my reasoning. Yelling, judging, and the weight of your extreme disappointment will only push your teen further away during this time. It's possible to express your lack of support for certain choices and enforce consequences while also sharing how much you love him or her and staying close to provide as much guidance and support as possible.

There's a well-known story about what some African tribes do when one of their members commits a crime. They bring that person into the town square, surround him or her in a big circle, and have everyone in the community tell that person all the wonderful things he or she has done. They take turns reminding the person how special and loved he or she is. They believe that all people are born good and perfect and when someone makes a mistake, it's not a sign of who he or she truly is, but rather an indication that the person needs to be reminded of his or her uniquely beautiful talents and gifts.

Our therapist told us that when our son was acting out in ways that were abhorrent to us, we needed to first make it clear that we did not approve, then impose the appropriate consequences (calmly — no yelling or hitting), and then shower him with love and reminders of all of his strengths and positive qualities. We were encouraged to spend lots of time with him, play games, ask him to help with projects, even try to laugh and have fun as much as possible. There was plenty of opportunity to do this since he was regularly grounded. We were told to keep home and family a warm, safe place, even if there was zero tolerance for certain choices. You can do both. I promise, you really can. It worked for us. Our son is so well adjusted and balanced now. We all came through it and I credit this approach, which we learned from our therapist, with our survival through that stage.

6. BONUS FUN TIP: LET GO AND PLAY!

Enjoy yourself and have fun when you're with kids. Laugh with them. Be silly with them. It's essential for them and for you! If you don't have children of your own, please provide breaks for friends and family members who do and you'll reap countless rewards, I assure you! Yes, spending time with kids can be exhausting and labor-intensive. But if you let go of wanting everything to be perfect, children can be the most amazing teachers for adults. They show us how to play and laugh and seek adventure with abandon. Take them to a playground and join in the fun, tossing your head back to look up at the sky on the swing, making castles in the sand, spinning in circles until you collapse with dizziness, rolling down grassy hills.

Children remind us to live in the present moment. Don't get so angry when that four-year-old refuses to put on his coat when it's cold outside because he's so engrossed in his building blocks. Consider the possibility that you're spending too much time planning for the next moment rather than relishing the joy of the here and now. Maybe it's really not so important to get out the door right this minute and you can allow your little four-year-old Zen

53

master a few more minutes of precious playtime. Then watch him and learn how to make your own life so, so much better.

The Bottom Line:

1. Listen to kids. You'll learn a lot and give them a rare gift.
2. Teach important lessons with words and logical reasoning, not force.
3. Speak softly. Yelling may not hurt physically, but it causes emotional wounds.
4. Model respectful conflict resolution rather than fighting in front of kids.
5. Forgive teenagers their need to rebel. Love them through this confusing time.
6. Play with children to learn to be present and to experience unadulterated joy.

CHAPTER 5

COMMUNICATING WITH DIFFERENT PERSONALITY TYPES

1. APPRECIATE THAT YOUR WAY ISN'T THE ONLY WAY

Have you ever watched someone do something and thought to yourself, "That's weird, why would he/she do it that way?" Have you ever heard someone make a statement and reacted in horror at what a strange or inappropriate thing it was to say? And let's be honest, how many times in a week do you find yourself noticing that someone is wrong or mistaken or rude or strange? Forgive me for saying this in such a blunt way, please, but what I need for you to know is that the problem is actually you, not any of those other people or how they do things. You are the problem and you always have been. The reason you are the problem is that you have your fixed way of doing and seeing things and when others don't conform to what you think is right, you judge them, dismiss them, curse them... or worse. How do I know that you do this? Because I do it too. We all do. It's human nature. The good news is that there are ways to get past this ugly, limiting part of our nature. One of them is to learn about different personality types and work to value all of them — especially those most dissimilar to our own.

When I first attended a True Colors® training session long ago, as a participant, I was already a university lecturer and corporate trainer. So I was familiar with many well-known personality tests and had taken several of them, including the DISC® assessment and the Myers-Briggs Type Indicator (MBTI®). Myers-Briggs was particularly meaningful for me because it helped me understand that I'm right in the middle of being an extrovert and an introvert, rather than being one extreme or the other. I showed up at the True Colors® training expecting more of the same: what I got instead was the answer to a calling I didn't even know existed until that day.

You see, I've always been fascinated by people, all people. I love learning about their histories, their thoughts, their fears, and their choices — regardless of how similar to or different from mine they may be. I want to know everything about what makes people tick. Why do some people yearn to travel the world while others have no desire to ever leave the small town they live in? How is it that some of my friends always have every item in their homes in perfect order while up until last week the contents of my overstuffed kitchen junk drawer included coupons that were more than four years old? Why is it that some people dive into romance, fully expressing their love early and often, while others show great restraint and patience, taking things slow and making choices based on reason rather than passion? If you're curious about why I said "up until last week," in reference to the disarray of my kitchen junk drawer, I must give credit to Marie Kondo and her book, *The Life-Changing Magic of Tidying Up: The Japanese Art of Decluttering and Organizing*, for freeing me from my enslavement to unnecessary possessions and clutter. Although being tidy and organized is definitely not an innate part of my nature, we all have the potential to grow and learn new strategies for overcoming our shortcomings.

True Colors® answered many of the above questions and more for me. I fell in love with it immediately and the love affair has raged on for over ten years now. I am a certified True Colors® trainer. I am always happy to share True Colors® with anyone interested because it transformed my life by showing me how to leverage my strengths and improve all my relationships. In this chapter, I'll only be able to provide a brief introduction to the four colors so I strongly suggest that you read more about them by exploring truecolorsintl.com and checking out the many books about True Colors®. You might also want to hire me or another certified facilitator to lead a True Colors® session for any team you're part of to improve teamwork and minimize conflict.

The next four tips will be dedicated to understanding and communicating with each of the four primary colors. But I must explain a bit about True Colors® first. There is a long, rich history of study spanning a wide range of disciplines such as medicine, psychology, sociology, and more, to prove that there are unique and distinguishable personality types. This is not astrology or Tarot card reading. True Colors® is founded on solid scholarship and has the same legitimate credentials as any of the other personality or talent assessment instruments you may be familiar with.

Every person is made up of all four colors, but some are more dominant and come more naturally. I am a blue, green, gold, orange. That's what is known as my color spectrum. After learning their True Colors®, people will usually refer to their first color mainly. But this is an incomplete picture. As a blue green, I am very different from a blue gold or a blue orange. The fact that orange is my last color is as important a part of my unique personality as the fact that blue is my first. In addition to that, when I take the True Colors® word cluster test, I score 24 out of 24 possible points in blue. So I'm a very blue blue. Every description of the blue personality should have my picture next to it. Another person might be primarily blue, but could have scored 20 out of 24 in blue and a higher number than I have in the second color. So there would be marked differences in our preferences, styles, etc. because of the distribution of all our possible points.

No number in any color or order of colors is better than any other. We are all equally unique and talented. Unfortunately, some don't find themselves in the most nurturing environments so they never realize their true potential. True Colors® reinforces our natural skill sets and teaches us how those abilities can complement the talents that others possess. Also, when we choose to value the unique gifts of others rather than trying to make everyone just like us, life becomes so much more pleasant.

After administering the True Colors® word cluster assessment to thousands of people over the years, I can confidently say that if one takes the test and feels the results are inaccurate, the problem is with the individual, not the assessment. The process simply involves selecting which clusters of adjectives best describe you and which least describe you. You pick them. The test results are all up to you. No one chooses your color spectrum for you. You decide based on which qualities you identify with most. Then those same qualities are reflected back to you in the descriptions of each primary color. If the explanation of your primary color feels inaccurate to you, you'll have to ask yourself why you selected all the adjectives that describe that color as being most like you. Pretty much every time I've facilitated a True Colors® training session and someone tried to argue that the test was faulty, it was because they either lacked self-awareness, were struggling with their own identity (often because someone had made them feel they weren't good enough), or were still working through a current or past crisis. Yes, I'm a bit defensive about True Colors® because I've seen it empower and inspire so many people to be proud of who they are and make the most of their talents.

Though I strongly advise that you take the True Colors® assessment, even if you don't, it's likely that you'll recognize yourself and others in the descriptions below. You may be able to identify your own color spectrum and those of people you know well. Please remember that my ultimate goal here is to get you to see that people have many different personalities, strengths, and preferences, and they should all be equally valued. I want you to stop thinking everyone should be like you and celebrate all that you can learn from the incredible diversity of the people in your life.

2. SHOW GREENS LOGIC

Just as I scored the highest possible number in blue, my husband consistently does the same in green. Combine that with the fact that green is my second color, and you can see why I have great insight into the green personality. Greens are thinkers. They are contemplative and enjoy chewing on ideas and theories. Many greens read a lot and extensively research the subjects they're interested in or the pros and cons of various brands before purchasing a product, sometimes to the point of analysis paralysis — the inability to make a final decision. Other greens may mull over complex ideas and philosophies in their own mind. Greens tend to enjoy solving problems and are prone to asking "why?" a lot. They don't ask "why?" to annoy or challenge you, so please don't take it that way. Understand that they are compelled to analyze things at a much deeper level than most people.

Greens are often intellectuals. They like to look at things from a calm, rational perspective. They aren't likely to display strong emotions, but that doesn't mean they don't feel them. One thing that bothers me about how people sometimes misunderstand True Colors® is when they suggest that greens are unfeeling or insensitive. This is not the case. My husband, for example, is loving, kind, and affectionate. He's just not likely to be that way in public and he wasn't quick to express those feelings early on. He preferred to play it cool until he was sure of his feelings and goals.

Because greens are usually highly intelligent and competence is very important to them, others may think they are overly critical. Again, the problem is not with greens, it's with those who take this part of their nature personally and don't realize that greens don't intend to be condescending. The phrase, "It's not about you" is important to repeat to yourself regularly when you deal with a green. I've learned to appreciate how my husband can always provide me with incredibly valuable feedback for improvement. He has the best ideas, suggestions, and ways to make anything better. This is common for greens. So, take advantage of their skill and knowledge rather than feeling attacked. Yes, greens can be perfectionists, and if their suggestions are too much for you, let them know. If you can communicate confidently with greens, while respecting and honoring what they've contributed, they are likely to appreciate anything you can teach them.

Greens are great students, which means if you logically explain a helpful new approach to something, a green is likely to eagerly apply the lesson and respect you forever after if it works well. And don't be surprised when you see that green doing the exact same thing in a relatively similar circumstance. Knowledge is power to greens and once they've acquired it, they love nothing more than to test it out in new situations. My husband once told me that he sees everything in life as either a puzzle to solve or a formula to figure out. Keep that in mind when you deal with greens.

To bring out the best in greens, ask for their advice, let them teach you what they know, and give them space to work and think independently. Stay calm and explain yourself rationally when you need to influence a green. Provide plenty of solid data. If you're in a romantic relationship with a green, don't assume that a lack of public display of affection means a lack of interest. Appreciate their smarts, their analytical skills, and their directness, rather than making them feel as if they're too critical, too rational, or too introspective.

In my workshops, after we've figured out everyone's True Colors®, I create teams of each primary color group and assign them a variety of tasks. One of them is to work together to create something out of a roll of party streamer in their primary color that represents their personality. Sometimes the green group refuses to do anything with their streamer because they see it as a silly, pointless exercise. I love when this happens because I can point out to the larger group that it has happened many times before and I don't take it personally at all but rather find it a fascinating illustration of the green mindset. Other times, greens will form the shape of a question mark, because they love to ask difficult questions. Another green favorite is E=MC^2.

3. SHOW BLUES LOVE

When I first found out I was a blue, I was elated. It made me so happy to learn that True Colors® had nothing but positive, affirming descriptions of my personality type. Now it makes me laugh to realize what a blue reaction that was. Blues feel things deeply. They are communicators and caretakers. Blues are peaceful, passionate, and enjoy doing anything they can to help others. We are often heartbroken by stories of injustice or any kind of cruelty to animals and children.

Blues naturally serve as mediators when there is conflict. They can see all sides of an issue and want to try to get everyone else to see all perspectives. Blues usually enjoy collaborative work because they are so people-oriented. Freedom of expression, creativity, authenticity, and love are often core values for blues. They usually have a variety of causes that they feel compelled to donate time and money to, if possible.

Most blues are comfortable sharing their emotions and communicating openly about almost all issues. They tend to have strong bonds with people, especially other blues. My closest friends are mostly blues, though I push myself to build my relationships with all primary colors because we have so much to learn from one another. Again, a very blue thing to do.

Understand that blues may have a difficult time engaging in conversations that are hostile or combative. Allow them to express their thoughts and feelings with minimal judgment in response when possible. Though blues are not likely to initiate arguments often, because their emotions reside close to the surface, they may on rare occasions lash out in anger when they witness some kind of injustice. When I've done this, I almost always regret it later and wish I'd handled the situation with more diplomacy. Blues tend to be even harder on themselves for unkind communication or choices than they are on others.

Please don't think you need to walk on eggshells with blues because you believe they're too sensitive. They appreciate honest communication. Sometimes when people learn that I'm a blue, they mistakenly take me for a pushover. Always remember that a person's second color joins with the first to create a unique combination. For example, I am regularly required to set aside my blue traits and bring my green qualities to the forefront as an instructor and coach. I can be as demanding, direct, and challenging as most strong greens when I need to be.

To bring out the best in blues, do what you can to make the environment supportive, harmonious, and cooperative. Listen to blues and share how you feel with them, to the degree that you're comfortable. They tend to be active listeners. Offer blues opportunities to help, encourage, and uplift you. However, please don't take advantage of their generosity without showing appreciation, because being told that they've helped in some way is important to blues. Value and praise their kindness, their genuineness, and their generosity rather than making them feel that they are too sensitive, too talkative, too nice.

For the streamer exercise, blues almost always make hearts, peace symbols, and happy faces. Almost always, I swear. They also often ask for little bits of the other color streamers to add to their creation so they can show how much they love and value all the colors of the human rainbow. Just yesterday, in a True Colors® workshop I facilitated, the blue group made necklaces out of their streamer and hand delivered one to each of the participants in the class as a gift. We are hopeless bleeding hearts, I know. Love us anyway, please.

4. SHOW GOLDS DEPENDABILITY

Gold is my third color and despite my years of teaching people that no color is better than any other, I still struggle with gold envy. Golds are natural organizers and planners. They are great with detail-oriented tasks and almost never forget important dates. Golds value follow-through and timely completion. They tend to be well prepared in any situation and their loyalty and dedication to the things they commit themselves to is unshakable. Golds have an innate ability to create systems and structures that the rest of us rely on to keep our lives somewhat together.

If gold is not your primary or secondary color, I recommend doing as I've done and giving in to allowing golds to do the planning and organizing of events and activities. They are better at it than the rest of us and they usually want to do it. We shouldn't take this too far though by assigning them all the work. Though they are highly capable of making sure every i is dotted and t crossed, whether it be a work project or family reunion, we all have our limits and appreciate a little help. Let golds delegate the work for you: they likely know better than you do what you're good at and what you're not so good at.

It's important not to stereotype people based on their primary color. While some might think golds are rigid and no fun, I've had quite a wild time with a gold or two on many occasions. In fact, they are sometimes the very people who need our encouragement to let loose and have fun and not always be the one who takes care of everyone else. Just because certain behaviors and abilities come naturally for us, doesn't mean we don't enjoy playing in every color some of the time!

To bring out the best in golds, acknowledge their stellar organization and planning skills and allow them to take control when they want to, because they will do a better job than you or I will, I promise. Make sure tasks and details are very clear, whatever the situation may be. Ambiguity can stress us all out, but especially golds. They are rarely late and like others to be on time too so it's worth leaving a few minutes early to make them happy, even if it doesn't seem that important to you. Understand that golds like to plan things in advance and like to have all the details figured out. Don't make them wait too long for a response or be wishy-washy about decisions. Appreciate their follow-through, their efficiency, and their leadership, rather than making them feel as if they're too rigid, too structured, or too demanding.

I have way more gold streamers leftover than any other color from all my True Colors® training sessions. Why? The gold group very frequently tells me that they decided not to do anything with the streamer because it would be wasteful. They hand it back to me intact and encourage me to save it to use at my next training. This is so gold. Golds don't like waste and they like to provide helpful, practical suggestions and resources. If they do use a bit of the streamer, it's usually to create a clock to remind people to be on time or a neat border for another part of the group exercise, which requires them to list their top values and frustrations.

5. SHOW ORANGES EXCITEMENT

Orange is my last color. I have to confess that I've tried to increase my orange score many times over the years, to no avail. I so want to be more orange. I do believe I have become more orange, thanks to my orange friends and colleagues. I actually think we can strengthen each color and push out of our comfort zone to grow in our third and fourth colors. Does that mean our colors will change their order? It's not likely. But we can become MORE of each color to experience a full, rewarding life. We can learn from those who are different from us if we're open to it.

Oranges are adventurous, playful, risk-takers. They are the people in my True Colors® training sessions who love to talk about their sky diving and bungee jumping experiences. They not only welcome change, they crave it. Many an orange has shared a story about rearranging their entire home on a whim because they were bored with it or calling all their friends to see who would be up for a last-minute road trip to Vegas.

Oranges want an action-packed life filled with surprises and new challenges. They are usually very confident and outgoing. They like to have fun and want everyone else to have fun too. They tend to dislike too much structure and order. Oranges don't want to be told what to do or how to do it. They need lots of freedom to do things their own way. Oranges also tend to be good at multitasking and doing things quickly. A tight deadline is likely to motivate an orange.

Though I always get the lowest score in orange, I can relate to oranges in many ways. Please don't take True Colors® too far and assume that any two people are so different that the gap can't be bridged. It always can.

Happy friendships, love relationships, and professional partnerships are entirely possible no matter how opposite our True Colors® results may be. Blue is my husband's last color. But he lets his blue shine through for me because he knows how much it means to me. I can relate to oranges because I love to have fun with other people. I also like to be challenged. I stand up for oranges all the time. I don't like it when people suggest that they are unfocused or uncooperative. I think we need to see the positive in others. We can choose to see oranges as rule-breakers or we can choose to see them as innovative visionaries unbound by outdated structures.

To bring out the best in oranges, give them ample freedom to explore, experiment, and push through boundaries. Let them do things their own way and don't stress them out with tasks that require repetition or sticking too closely to a particular protocol. Appreciate their creativity, their energy, and their confidence, rather than making them feel as if they're too impulsive, too unstable, or too fidgety.

It's always the most fun to watch the interesting things oranges do with their streamer during the group exercises. They often turn it into a toy, tossing it around and unraveling it all with great joy. I am forever buying more orange streamer. Oranges like to live life to the fullest and use anything they're given, soaking up every bit of joy they can squeeze out of it. Orange groups have decorated the entire room with their streamer to make it feel more lively and they often wear it all over their bodies to proudly add splashes of orange to their attire.

6. BONUS FUN TIP: HANG OUT WITH ORANGES MORE OFTEN

I apologize to oranges for the fact that this tip is for all groups but theirs. But chances are that oranges naturally have no shortage of fun in their lives. The rest of us should be making every effort to spend as much time as possible with oranges to lighten up our lives and have a great time. Oranges are the life of the party — so make sure you invite them to your gatherings! Oranges will crack a joke in a meeting at just the right time to break the tension and help everyone relax. Oranges will push you out of your comfort zone, nudging you to try things you'd never do on your own, which you may discover you actually enjoy. Analyze your circle of friends right now and make sure there is a strong orange presence. If there isn't, it's time to make some new friends who will enrich your life in ways you can't possibly imagine... if you let them.

The Bottom Line:

1. **Get over yourself and the notion that your way is always the right way.**
2. **Adapt to greens with information, thorough analysis, and rationality.**
3. **Adapt to blues with open communication, appreciation, and kindness.**
4. **Adapt to golds with order, dependability, and loyalty.**
5. **Adapt to oranges with flexibility, enthusiasm, and play.**
6. **Blues, greens, and golds should call on oranges to help them lighten up.**

CHAPTER 6

COMMUNICATING WITH AN AUDIENCE

1. CONQUER THE FEAR WITH KNOWLEDGE AND PRACTICE

My first speech in my undergraduate speech class was a disaster. I don't recall what my topic was but I know I only lasted for about three of the required five minutes before ending my speech early to slink back to the safety of my desk. My teacher was generous enough to give me a low C grade. I had been a wreck all week, barely able to eat or sleep as I envisioned horrific scenarios involving forgetting my entire speech, fainting in front of the class, and my classmates all rolling on the floor laughing at me.

Thankfully, with the support and information I received from my wonderful speech teacher as well as plenty of practice, by the end of the semester I felt confident and excited about delivering my persuasive speech on recycling. I received a high A on that one. In those short fifteen weeks, I learned how to research and organize my points, how to deliver a speech with poise, and how to keep my nervousness under control. Anyone can do this. You can do this. If you find it hard to believe that one basic speech class transformed my public speaking skills so dramatically, consider this: it was my only undergraduate class focusing solely on speech, yet just a little over two years after taking it, I was teaching it.

Experts estimate that about 75% of people fear public speaking. Psychologists label this fear an irrational fear. It's irrational because the emotional and physical response people often experience before and during public speaking — extreme anxiety, shaking, sweating, dizziness, etc. — are more in line with something like having a gun to your head than having to simply communicate your thoughts with a few more people than you're used to doing it with. The things we fear about public speaking situations almost never actually happen. In twenty-five years of teaching public speaking, with some truly terrified young people in my classes, I have never had a student faint, vomit, forget their speech (having a brief outline prevents that anyway), had students laugh at them, or any of the other ridiculous things we all fear.

In hindsight, I realize that during that traumatic first speech of mine, the other students were more likely stressing out about their own speeches than paying any attention to mine. The truth is that when you are the speaker, your audience wants you to do well. They want to hear what you have to share. They empathize with how hard it is to get up in front of a group of people to express your thoughts. If you can control your irrational fears and realize that the people present are there to support you, hear you, and that they do not expect your speech to be perfect, you should be able to calm your fears substantially.

It's not desirable to go into a speech without any nervousness at all. People who are too relaxed don't tend to be high-energy speakers. A little anxiety pumps you up. It also means you have a desire to do well, to make a good impression. Someone who couldn't care less about the response to his or her presentation isn't likely to put the necessary effort into impressing the audience.

If you feel nervous before a speech, remind yourself that it's normal and good to feel that way. If you have physical symptoms, ignore them. Drawing attention to them and focusing on them makes them worse. Don't announce that you're nervous because most people are much better at hiding it than they think. Giving away your nervousness by stating it makes listeners much more aware of it. Focus on your message. You don't have to be Dr. Martin Luther King Jr. You just have to be yourself. The best speakers have learned that while they need to be articulate and poised, they will have the most impact when they are genuine, conversational, and let their natural personality shine through. The same is true for you.

Knowledge and practice are proven to be the top two ways to conquer the fear of public speaking. In the next few points, I'll share most of what you need to know to be a great speaker. Getting practice is up to you. You can take a class, you can join Toastmasters International, or you can find opportunities to practice your public speaking skills at your job, your school, community organizations, your place of worship, etc. Graciously accept any invitation to speak, and offer your speaking services for pay or just to help out as much as possible.

2. GIVE UP YOUR EXPECTATION OF PERFECTION

Be warned that no matter how much you study public speaking or how much practice you get, you'll never be perfect! It's not possible. Stumbling over a word, a few ums (just a few — practice helps reduce those), dropping your notes, fumbling with uncooperative technology, and many other unexpected glitches are to be expected and are entirely forgivable if you don't make a big deal out of them.

One time, on the very first day of class, my nerves got the better of me as I was setting up my computer at the front of the room, with all my new students watching me. So concerned about what they might be thinking of me, I didn't pay attention to the computer cord as I tripped over it, almost falling to the floor, but catching myself in time. My laptop wasn't so lucky. It was pulled across the front desk and slammed onto the floor as my students sat in shocked horror. I had no choice but to look at them and say with a nonchalant shrug of my shoulders, "Hope it still works. I really like the PowerPoint slides I created for you today." My new students felt nothing but concern for me and for my laptop, which survived its fall, thankfully. The rest of the class went off without a hitch. So don't expect perfection. Whatever happens, stay calm, make the best of it and remember that most people in any audience are generally kind, forgiving of small mistakes, and want you to succeed. For the people who don't fit into that category, who cares what they think anyway?

Perfectionism is one of the greatest obstacles to learning through trial and error. Perfectionism is also a great way to increase the chances that you'll live an unfulfilled life. When we don't step out of our comfort zones to take risks despite the possibility of failure, we don't grow. In fact, it's best to believe that there is no such thing as failure. When something doesn't turn out as we had hoped, we can choose to learn from that experience and try different choices in the future.

I still mess up as a speaker and in other areas of my life. I've made mistakes in my career and personal life. One of the reasons I live fully and get to do and experience things other people want to but never get to is because I'm willing to put myself out there with the full knowledge that I won't do it perfectly. When we take risks to go after what we want, things may not turn out as planned, but we almost always come away with something more than we had before. Please consider taking more risks in your life, especially with your communication choices.

I've had many students share with me that after conquering their fear of public speaking, and getting good at it, even though they could never be perfect, they felt they could do anything. They were suddenly able to muster up the confidence to break up with that demeaning partner or able to stand up to that family member who always told them they'd never amount to anything. Doing something well or even just okay because you took the risk to try it is better than avoiding the risk because you may not do it perfectly. Having this mindset with regard to public speaking as well as most of the rest of the challenges in life will take you far.

3. GIVE 'EM WHAT THEY NEED, WHAT THEY WANT, AND MORE

At one level there's the topic you've been asked to speak about, but with a little imagination you can take it to a higher level. There are all sorts of ways to get creative with your subject matter so that your listeners will feel that they gained much more than they ever expected from your talk.

I just finished teaching a section of organizational communication on Friday mornings from 8:00 am to 10:45 am and was very touched by the feedback I got from a number of students. Much of it reflected what I'm trying to say here. One student posted this on Facebook, along with a picture of the two of us at her graduation a few days ago: "Professor Sampson was one of my favorite professors at CSUN, hands down! She is so supportive of her students and wants nothing more than to see us happy and successful. Thank you for everything you have taught me!" Yes, it was my job to make sure my students learned the relevant theories of organizational communication, but I also made it my job to do all I could to teach my students how to be happy and successful in their lives. Another student gave me a card on the last day that said, "Every Friday at 10:45, I leave your class amped up with motivation to inspire me to be a better person." To me, that's about the best thing a student could possibly say about the lessons learned in one of my classes. Any subject I'm asked to speak about will cover that topic and much more. Make it your goal to do the same when you're the speaker.

To figure out what that "something more" should be, you have to put yourself in the place of your audience and ask yourself who they are, where they are in their lives, and what you could share with them that would be most meaningful, helpful, and inspiring. Don't do this at the expense of thoroughly covering the required subject, rather, find a way to build it into your topic. It's possible with any subject. I've been able to do it with everything from sales training to financial planning talks, so don't try to tell me you can't do it with your speeches.

4. GET ORGANIZED

I know I said earlier that most people in your audience are forgiving and want you to succeed. But if you don't at least do the bare minimum to organize your thoughts and points before speaking to them, they may get frustrated by how difficult it is to follow you. Prevent this problem by planning and outlining your speech. Even if you only take five minutes to pull together a rough outline of key points, you'll be much more likely to stay on track and avoid irrelevant, annoying tangents. When the opening doesn't provide the audience with a clear picture of the purpose of the speech, where it's going, and why it's important, there's a great risk of losing the audience. After all, there are so many ways to check out during a speech. People can pull out their smartphones and other gadgets to check email, play Words With Friends, or jot down their shopping list. If you've got great content (see #3) and are well organized, the chances are high that your audience will respond well to your speech, even if you're nervous and don't have the most dynamic delivery.

The outline format I recommend is one I've formulated based on the basic frameworks I've learned from the many public speaking textbooks I've used over the years. In public speaking training sessions, I provide a one-page outline template with a box for each of the points I believe are required for a good speech. It's important to be sure to just jot down a few key words in each section, not long sentences or paragraphs. Too many words may tempt you to read from the outline, which is not a good idea.

The introduction should include four main elements, in the following order: an attention grabber, a statement of the topic and why it's important, a mention of your credibility, and a preview of main points. Grab the audience's attention with an interesting story, a surprising statistic, a provocative question, or something else along those lines. They will make up their minds in the first few seconds of your speech about whether or not you're worth listening to, so the attention grabber is not a step to skip.

The attention grabber should lead right into a clear statement of the topic and why it's important. This could be as brief as one or two sentences. Don't get into the details until you get to the body of the speech. The introduction should be short and sweet. After you've clearly stated your subject and why the audience should care about it, make a brief mention of what makes you an expert on the subject. Finally, quickly preview the main points you'll cover in the body of the speech. Why do you have to do this when it seems redundant? Research says the average listener will forget roughly 75 to 90% of what you said forty-eight hours after your talk. Pretty sad, right? So, if you at least preview and review your key points, there's a better chance your listeners will remember them!

Here's a sample introduction, but remember I do not recommend writing things out word for word, so I'll show you how it might sound, then how I might outline it before the speech. Let's say I'm giving a talk on being a communication consultant for communication studies majors. My introduction might sound something like this: *How would you like a career that allows you to control your own schedule, change people's lives for the better, and travel the world? Well that's what being a communication consultant has done for me and I want to help you figure out if it might be right for you. I've been a consultant for over twenty years, working with companies from small nonprofits to corporate giants such as Google. The key points I'll go over today are the recommended education, the personal qualities necessary, and how you can prepare to become a consultant.*

The outline for my introduction might look something like this:

- schedule, lives, travel
- comm consult, for you?
- 20 yrs.
- education, qualities, preparation

I would likely also have interesting images on PowerPoint slides, such as photographs of travel for the attention grabber, company logos for the credibility statement, a picture of a very enthusiastic person when I mention personal qualities, etc.

For the body of your speech, organize your content into three main points if you can. If you can't, two is okay and four can work, but more than that creates a serious risk of people forgetting one or two of the key points. Make sure your main points are covered for a relatively similar amount of time and that each has close to the same number of supporting points. Include a variety of interesting material within each point: research and data, personal stories and anecdotes, and concrete examples that people can relate to.

I must emphasize the importance of including personal stories in your talks. Your listeners want to relate to you as a human being. They want to know about you and your life as well as the topic you're covering. In one of my favorite new books on presentation skills, *Talk Like TED: The 9 Public-Speaking Secrets of the World's Top Minds*, author Carmine Gallo explains the powerful impact that stories have on audiences. He reveals that when brain researchers attached MRI sensors to audience members, they found that far more parts of the brain were activated and engaged while listening to a story than when hearing straight data and details. Even more compelling was the fact that the parts of the brain that were activated and emotions that were felt by audience members directly matched those of the speaker. So, telling a story is far more persuasive, impactful, and likely to stir the feelings you want to arouse in your listeners than just presenting them with the facts.

By this point, you could probably guess what my recommendations for the conclusion would be. This part is simple. There are three key steps: signal the end, review your topic and key points, and end with a bang. It can be awkward when a speaker ends abruptly without somehow signaling the end. There are all sorts of obvious words and phrases to choose from to indicate that you've entered the conclusion. The restatement of the topic and main points can usually be very concise. Then, end with something that leaves people thinking or moved in some way.

Here's a sample conclusion for my consulting speech: *So, I hope what I've shared gives you a better sense of what consulting is about and if it might be right for you. You now know more about the education you would need, the qualities that consultants tend to have, and how to start preparing for a consulting career. Whether you become a consultant or not, I urge you to follow your passion because, as Marc Anthony said, "If you do what you love, you'll never work a day in your life."*

5. POLISH YOUR DELIVERY SKILLS

The best way to figure out where you can improve your speech delivery is to record and watch yourself giving a talk. I know it's painful to do. I've had to do it and I certainly don't enjoy it. But nothing compares to seeing how you look and hearing how you sound if you truly want to get better. It's not as if avoiding it changes anything. Everyone else already sees and hears you, so why not face the truth about how you're coming across?

Eye contact is essential for public speakers. I ask my students to strive for eye contact with the audience 90% of the time while speaking. The other 10% can include quick glances at the brief outline for reminders. Eye contact also means that you are looking into the actual eyes of members of your audience. Unless you're speaking to an audience of thousands (and if you are, you probably don't need this chapter!), you will be close enough to your audience to make genuine eye contact with each of them several times. Looking above their heads or at their noses is not good advice. Try it and you'll see. It doesn't work.

Body movement should be kept to a minimum. Moving from one spot to another from time to time can help you connect with different parts of your audience, but doing it too many times is distracting. Don't shift your weight repeatedly. Keep your weight evenly grounded on both feet. Use your hands to gesture the way you naturally do. When you're not gesturing, find a comfortable position to rest your hands together at about waist level. Don't hold your hands behind your back, cross them in front of you, or let them dangle at your sides.

Don't speak too quickly or too slowly. Project your voice — be sure that your volume is loud enough to command the attention of everyone in the room. When you practice, make sure you have sufficient vocal variety. Nothing puts an audience to sleep quite like a monotone speaker. Make sure you sound enthusiastic, upbeat, and convey a sense of passion about whatever you're speaking about.

6. BONUS FUN TIP: WATCH TED TALKS AT TED.COM

The best speech content is anything the speaker feels passionate about and has experience with. The best speech delivery is eloquent, energetic, engaging, and genuine. Watch as many TED (technology, entertainment, and design) Talks as you can for samples of a wide variety of styles of speaking, all of which meet these criteria beautifully. Most TED Talks are only ten to twenty minutes long, yet are incredibly informative, entertaining, and inspiring.

The Bottom Line:

1. **Shed your irrational fear of public speaking through study and practice.**
2. **Stop expecting yourself to be perfect. You never will be. Just give it a go.**
3. **Always give your audience what they came for and more.**
4. **Use a brief outline, stay organized, and follow the tried-and-true steps.**
5. **Improve your delivery skills to become a more dynamic, impactful speaker.**
6. **Enjoy TED Talks regularly for inspiration and education.**

CHAPTER 7

COMMUNICATING WITH PEOPLE OF DIFFERENT CULTURES

1. KNOW THAT WHAT YOU BELIEVE IS "RIGHT" IS CULTURAL, NOT UNIVERSAL

A former student of mine contacted me for advice not long ago. She was grappling with the dilemma of whether or not to move in with her boyfriend. For the most part, she felt it would be the right thing for her to do at this point in her life. She admitted to having doubts, which I think is healthy anytime one has a big decision looming. In fact, many studies on decision-making have found that a belief that one choice is the absolute correct choice while all the others are wrong is unrealistic and may lead to great disappointment when the seemingly perfect choice doesn't live up to expectations.

But it wasn't this young woman's self-doubt that was causing her the greatest suffering. Let's call her Monica. At almost thirty, having just earned her college degree, Monica was relatively sure she wanted to move in with her boyfriend. It was her parents' reaction to the possibility that had left her stressed out and sleepless. Monica's mother told her that moving in with her boyfriend would ruin Monica's life and that her father would likely disown her as a result.

After teaching intercultural communication for a good many years, I am well aware of how ethnocentric most people are, myself included. From my cultural standpoint, there would be absolutely nothing wrong with Monica moving in with her boyfriend. I lived with my now husband for a year prior to marrying him and my American, liberal, slightly hippie-ish parents were nothing but supportive. It was hard not to feel frustrated with Monica's parents for making her feel so guilty.

But Monica is not my child and her parents are not my parents. Nor do we share the same culture or religion. What right do I have to suggest that what's considered appropriate in my family is also best for theirs? Monica's parents were raised to believe that it's unethical to cohabitate before marriage. They hoped to pass that belief on to their children. Don't all of us who are parents want our children to share our values and morality?

Would it have been unwise of me to tell Monica to ignore her parents' wishes and do whatever she wants? I think so. Instead, I tried to ask her questions to help her better understand where her parents were coming from and figure out how to engage in more productive, loving communication about the issue with them. Monica has decided to move forward with plans to live with her boyfriend. There is no big happy ending to the situation with her parents as of now, but Monica and I agree that all she can do is keep telling them how much she loves and appreciates them, understands how they feel, and wants very much to maintain a positive, close relationship with them.

2. LISTEN TO AND LEARN FROM THOSE WHO ARE CULTURALLY DIFFERENT FROM YOU

It's wonderful to be proud of your culture, ethnicity, heritage, race, religion, and all other aspects of your identity. But we must push back and use global, critical thinking skills when that pride crosses the line into ethnocentrism, the belief that our group is superior to others. Globalization has exposed people to diverse cultures like never before. We can see what's happening all over the world thanks to advances in technology and many of us can travel anywhere we like due to the increasing ease and affordability of various options for transportation.

Unfortunately, this increased exposure has not necessarily led to a significant increase in understanding and celebrating different cultures and practices. In some ways, globalization has led to cultures becoming more similar to one another, sometimes called the "McDonaldization" of world cultures. But many cultures resist this homogenization by reviving traditional cultural practices and rituals or resisting outside cultural influences. This pull between the forces nudging us all to be the same and the growing resistance advocating that cultures retain their uniqueness causes a great deal of intercultural conflict. What we can do to mitigate this challenge is work to engage with people who are different from us and truly listen to and learn from their experiences and perspectives, especially when they are significantly different from our own.

Every semester, in my intercultural communication course, international student panel speakers visit and share their experiences in their home countries compared with the United States. It's always an eye-opening experience for all of us. I'll never forget the time when a young woman shared her excitement about the arranged marriage she'd be going home to after completing her master's degree. "My parents love me so much and know me so well, I know they'll pick someone perfect for me. I'm so glad I don't have to worry about that myself," she gushed to the shocked crowd. Who am I, resident of one of the highest divorce rate states in the United States, to say that an arranged marriage doesn't have just as much potential for success as any other?

Many more of these epiphanies have occurred for me over the years, making me wonder how people of the world can interact with respect and treat each other as equals, given all their differences. A number of scholars have proposed universal communication ethics and they are worth considering. I particularly like one that has been suggested by David Kale: "The guiding principle of any universal code of intercultural communication should be to preserve the worth and dignity of the human spirit... it is unethical to communicate with people in a way that does violence to their concepts of themselves." I know that might seem vague, but I think it's a good place to start.

3. HAVE COMPASSION FOR THE DIFFICULTIES OF CULTURAL ADAPTATION

Have you ever traveled to a new country, where you didn't speak the language? Or perhaps you've moved to a new state or city, where everything seemed different from what you were used to. If so, you likely developed a greater awareness of how difficult it is. It can be very stressful to figure out how to do even the most simple things, such as finding food to your liking or locating a bathroom when you desperately need one.

When I hear people harshly criticizing immigrants for not learning the language, stealing jobs, and refusing to adopt the rules of the new culture, I am disheartened by the lack of compassion in our world. Many immigrants are forced to leave the countries and families they love in order to survive. They may have to flee oppressive regimes or religious persecution to protect their loved ones. In other cases, there is no choice but to seek opportunity in another land, not only for oneself but for all future generations who would otherwise face lives of destitution in their home country.

Can you imagine leaving the home and culture you love when you didn't want to, but had to, and then facing the judgment of members of the new culture who expect you to throw away everything that meant so much to you to become just like them immediately? It takes a long time to learn a new language. It is incredibly hard to adopt new behaviors and accept rules of interaction that go against everything that was ingrained in you in your home culture. We need to be patient and supportive when others are adapting to a new culture. We need to encourage them to find a balance between holding on to their own culture's cherished values while also integrating aspects of the new culture that are necessary for their ability to thrive.

Please don't engage in or condone arguments that blame immigrants for the ills of any country. As an American, I have deep respect for those who take great risks to come to my country seeking a better life for themselves and future generations of their families. I welcome them and the rich knowledge and experiences they bring to my country to share. I am also saddened by the exploitation of many immigrants who work long hours for almost no pay. We need to support much better minimum living standards for all people of the world.

A useful theory to help us understand the difficulties of being in an unfamiliar land, whether it be for a vacation or permanent residence, is the W curve model, created by Gullahorn and Gullahorn. The idea is that the top of the

W on the left represents the feelings we have about the prospect of traveling to a new culture. For example, many international students on a study abroad program who have been in my classes have shared that based on what they saw in the media and had heard about the United States, they envisioned an area such as Beverly Hills, with glamorous rich people, fancy cars, and high-end shops everywhere.

The arrival to a new culture often sparks the steady slide down the first line of the W to a disturbing low point, sometimes to the point of extreme disappointment or even fear. When we are suddenly in the new culture and it isn't what we expected, we may become upset and agitated. The international students I mentioned earlier have often shared with me the shock they felt seeing so many homeless people on the streets of Los Angeles. Nothing back home prepared them for such a disconcerting sight, one so contrary to the utopian "American Dream" they had been expecting. International travelers have also reported that though they may have studied English for years, speaking it in the United States, with native speakers who have different dialects, use many unfamiliar idioms, and speak very quickly, made them incredibly insecure about engaging in conversations.

As a person begins to get more comfortable with the language, where things are, how to behave, etc., he or she may climb back up to experiencing more positive feelings about being in the new culture. This is the top of the middle of the W. A person may begin to truly enjoy and even prefer aspects of the new culture when compared with his or her own. Many people from all over the world have told me that once they got the hang of how things work in the United States, they began to appreciate our freedom of expression and our diversity.

The second half of the W represents the potential for difficulty with re-entry adaptation to one's own culture. What can happen is that once a person is exposed to a new and very different culture, it may spark taking a more critical look at the practices and expectations of his or her home culture. I've heard, for example, that after experiencing the way the United States encourages people to look and act in unique ways that suit their individual preferences, it can be difficult to return home to countries where much more conformity is expected. But as the last line of the W suggests, the end of the process usually leaves us at the same level of satisfaction we started at, more or less. But, ideally, we are also much more well informed about other cultures as well as our own based on what we learned from our journey.

4. WHEN YOU VISIT A NEW COUNTRY/CULTURE, RESPECT AND ADAPT TO THEIR WAYS

Of all the places I've been so far, France is my favorite country to visit. I don't like it when people say that the French are rude and hate Americans. This has not been my experience. I'm also aware of the power of our expectations. Anytime you're expecting someone to act a certain way, you're more likely to treat that person in ways that draw out that behavior or attitude. I know that if I am kind, respectful, and try to treat people the way they are likely to wish to be treated, I will almost always be responded to in the same way. I also realize that what is viewed as kind and respectful may differ from culture to culture, so I must practice careful observation to pick up on cues about social norms and pay close attention to reactions to my approach.

The first time I was in Paris was for my honeymoon, twenty-three years ago. Though I had studied French in

87

school, shortly after arriving in Paris, a part of my initial W curve dip, as described above, was the realization that speaking French with actual French people was going to be much more difficult than I expected. I recall struggling through a long and frustrating conversation with the man at the front desk of our hotel. I stumbled and made one mistake after another as I asked questions about what time breakfast would be served, where the nearest Metro station was, and if we could have extra pillows. He was kind and friendly and spoke slowly in response to me, which helped to put me at ease.

When our conversation ended, as I was about to walk away, in perfect English he said, "It was very nice to meet you. Have a wonderful day." I looked at him with a stunned expression and asked him why he let me butcher his beautiful language for so long when he was clearly fluent in English and knew I was from the United States. He explained to me that he figured I needed the practice and that he truly appreciated the genuine attempt I was making to speak the language of his country. Then he said that it was very rare for any American to even attempt a basic conversation in French. Rather, they typically walked right up and began to pepper him with questions in English, not even bothering to ask if he speaks English first. I can understand why that might seem a bit disrespectful.

Our first dinner experience in Paris provided additional insights about the cultural norms. Being typical tourists, rather than be adventurous enough to try authentic French food right away, we ate at a pizza place. Famished from having walked around all day, we devoured our meal quickly and asked for the check. The manager appeared shortly after to ask us what his staff had done wrong. He seemed genuinely concerned and soundly convinced that we were unhappy with the service in his establishment. We were confused at first and unsure of what to say. I did my best to assure him that our pizza was très délicieux and that all was très bien, but he insisted on serving us a complimentary aperitif and dessert. We came to learn that it was a sign of displeasure to leave a restaurant too quickly. The French way is to sit and enjoy your meal very slowly, preferably savoring multiple courses. It wasn't difficult at all to embrace this new way of dining and by the end of the trip we found ourselves thoroughly enjoying sitting at a sidewalk cafe for hours.

I've been to France several times since that first memorable adventure. About a month ago, I was lucky enough to land a consulting gig involving work in London and Dublin, so I tacked on a weekend in Paris, where my husband met me for a romantic getaway. It was magical. Now knowing and loving the way the French enjoy life, we were prepared to adapt immediately and couldn't wait to do so. The hard part for me is coming home to the rushed pace of things (not to mention the inferior wine and cheese) back in the United States.

I don't mean to imply that all cultural differences are as easy to accept as how long you sit down for a meal. I am well aware that your values might clash with those of other countries in ways that present ethical dilemmas for you. In those cases, you'll have to figure out how to abide by cultural rules in ways you can live with, at least temporarily. For instance, I have friends who regularly travel to countries where it's required for a woman's head to be covered. Though they may not agree with the practice, these women understand that if they choose to visit those countries, they must abide by the rule.

My personal examples of cultural adaptation reveal my privilege as a person who is in a position to choose where I find myself in the world. This is not the case for many individuals. People such as refugees, immigrants fleeing oppressive conditions, and young people who may commute from an inner-city community to a college campus are faced with countless challenges as they struggle to figure out the new rules of engagement. For example, my college students who grew up in South Los Angeles were socialized into particular speech patterns and styles of language use, which are quite different from the norms expected and rewarded in an academic setting. These students often find it difficult to alter the way they speak to meet the expectations of professors, potential employers, etc. Certain ways of speaking English based on European American middle-class norms are coded as "standard" and "acceptable," while other ways of speaking are judged as indicators of inferior intelligence or capabilities. While my students quickly realize this, and work hard to change the way they speak, there is often little recognition by those in the dominant culture of the additional work students from non-dominant communities have to engage in to code switch as they navigate academic environments.

5. ADMIT THAT RACISM, DISCRIMINATION, AND UNEQUAL OPPORTUNITIES EXIST AND FIGHT FOR THOSE WHO HAVE LESS PRIVILEGE THAN YOU

While I find it extremely rewarding, one of the frustrating things about teaching intercultural communication is that when we discuss racism and other forms of injustice, a small percentage of students sometimes challenge the idea that these problems still exist. Individuals who are in the privileged categories of their culture may not realize the realities of what others, who are less privileged, experience.

There is a show called "What Would You Do?" hosted by John Quinones, on ABC, that uses hidden cameras to capture people's reactions to a variety of situations. One episode involved having teenage actors pretend to be vandalizing a car in the parking lot of a neighborhood park. The experiment was done twice, first with a group of white teens and then with a group of black teens. All other factors were exactly the same — the location, the car type, the numbers of people passing by, the length of time the alleged vandalism took place for, etc. You can imagine where I'm going with this, right? There were ten calls to 911 about the black teens, while there was only one call when the white teens were engaged in the same alleged criminal act. Not only that, but while the white teens were supposedly vandalizing a car, in another part of the parking lot, the black teens were napping in a different car. Two calls were made to 911 about them, because though they were simply sleeping, it was assumed that they were getting ready to do something illegal. You might want to argue that the show's footage could have been edited in misleading ways, but after many years of listening to the stories of my students of color, I can assure you there is no doubt that this kind of thing happens all the time.

It's not just blatantly racist, ignorant people who make these kinds of faulty or biased assumptions and discriminate in this way. Even peace-loving, equality-advocating, educated individuals are prone to making the same mistakes. It's the way we're conditioned. We see certain races on the news more often as suspects. Then we forget to ask whether race is really the connection or poverty is. One is more likely to steal or engage in petty crimes when resources and opportunities in life are scarce. It's not about race. But in a different way, it is about race, not because certain races are more prone to be criminals, but because certain races are more likely to be born poor and to not have access to a decent education or job. As I mentioned in the chapter on communicating with yourself, close to one in three black and Latino babies are born into poverty in the United States while about one in ten white children are. Similar statistics demonstrate the disparities between privileged and underprivileged groups in countless other categories. Substandard living conditions and rights for minority races and ethnicities are found worldwide and simply cannot be denied if one takes an honest look at the facts.

Studies show that discrimination in hiring, housing, and education happens regularly. Unearned privileges and advantages are passed on from generation to generation for the same groups, while other groups struggle to get by. There was an article in the *Wall Street Journal* a while back about affirmative action for rich kids. The article exposed the prevalence of rich kids being accepted to elite universities though their qualifications fall far short of the minimum requirements. They were granted admission not based on merit, but because their parents were expected to be major donors. Similar exceptions are made regularly for children of alumni or powerful people and many more groups that are often already privileged in a variety of ways, such as skin color. Yet, when a university wants to give a hard-working, disadvantaged student of color a few extra admissions points, a stir is often created about how unfair that is to deserving white kids who didn't get those few extra points. The hypocrisy drives me crazy.

I am a proponent of affirmative action to remedy past and present discriminatory laws and practices. But I find that most people misunderstand what affirmative action is. If two people are relatively equally qualified for an opportunity, and one is from a group that has been historically disadvantaged and the other is from a group that has been historically privileged, I believe the opportunity should go to the former. I say this as a white person who has lived a pretty privileged life and knows it. I have seen others have to work much harder and overcome far more obstacles than I have to reach the same place, and so I would happily extend my hand to let them walk before me, congratulating them on overcoming great odds. I also know we have to rethink some of our methods for measuring who is qualified. How fair is it that my son got a high SAT score, in part, because we paid for a long and pricey prep class? It's not fair at all. Of course I wanted my son to have the best chances of getting into a good college, but I'm sure the mother thirty minutes away whose son went to an inner-city public high school and who can't afford that prep class, wanted the same for her son. His score might have been just as high if he had the means our family has.

Because I am well aware of the vast inequities in our educational system, our organizations' hiring and promotion practices, and even everyday courtesies such as receiving prompt, pleasant service in a retail establishment, I make it my mission to fight for those who have less than I have. As I've mentioned before, I have worked for the Educational Opportunity Program at California State University, Northridge for many years, helping students who come from low-income backgrounds and are the first in their families to go to college. My husband and I donate money to scholarships, foster youth advocacy programs, and other causes that help those who have not been given a fair shot in life. We volunteer regularly for similar programs. I believe it's up to all of us to lift others up to what I hope might eventually become a truly equal playing field one day, but we have a very, very long way to go before that happens.

I must take a moment to give credit to one of my most beloved mentors, because she has informed and shaped many of the opinions I've expressed in this chapter. The current Chair of the Communication Studies department at CSUN, Kathryn Sorrells, is the author of what I consider to be the most superior intercultural communication textbook that exists, by far. She focuses on globalization and social justice and I wish I could share more of what I've learned from her here. If you appreciate the tips in this chapter, you might want to consider ordering her textbook to read yourself. Not only do I use her book in my classes, I have read it several times as well as recording myself reading the entire book on the voice memo program on my phone so that I can listen to it over and over. It only took me about an hour to read each chapter aloud, which allows me to re-listen to chapters while exercising, doing chores, etc., and has helped me integrate the material into my mind at a much deeper level than just reading it possibly could. I highly recommend this recording practice when you want to burn important lessons into your soul, rather than reading them once and then forgetting them, as we so often do.

6. BONUS FUN TIP: TRAVEL THE WORLD

If you have the means, please take every opportunity to explore new places. When you travel, don't stick to tourist locations. Visit small towns and places that are off the beaten path to get a better sense of how members of the culture live. Eat the local food rather than seeking out the same cuisine you eat at home. Thanks to globalization, you can find familiar fast-food establishments in almost every country. Personally, I wouldn't patronize them at home or abroad. As I sit here, I can almost taste the pillows of scrumptious homemade gnocchi that melted in my mouth in a tiny out-of-the-way village in Italy.

I realize that not everyone has the funds or ability to travel. If this is the case, you can still explore the regions of the world that intrigue you as long as you have access to a computer. My family and I are currently preparing for a trip to England, Scotland, and Ireland. So I've been searching YouTube for videos about places to see in those countries and have been amazed at how many there are. You can travel almost anywhere you like virtually, and though it may not be the same as going to those places, it's a free alternative to expose yourself to new cultures and help you see all the rich diversity and beauty the world has to offer.

The Bottom Line:

1. **Admit to your own ethnocentrism and wage war against it.**
2. **Listen to the histories and experiences of those who are different from you.**
3. **Understand how difficult cultural adaptation is and make it easier if you can.**
4. **Learn and adapt to the norms and expectations of the cultures you visit.**
5. **Do not deny or minimize the injustices of the past and present. Advocate for all.**
6. **Learn from traveling the world yourself or seeing it through the eyes of others.**

CHAPTER 8

COMMUNICATING WITH PEOPLE YOU LEAD, TEACH, OR MENTOR

1. TREAT THEM AS EQUALS

Being in a position of power over others — as their boss, their teacher, the president of an organization, etc. — does not mean you are better than them or that they don't deserve your respect. Position power used to hold a lot of weight for leaders. You could throw your title around and people had to do what you said, regardless of whether or not it made sense or seemed reasonable. Today, leaders can't get away with that approach and I see that as a very good thing. As a consultant for over two decades, I've witnessed a huge shift in leadership training. Being in charge used to mean directing, controlling, and critiquing. Now it means mentoring, inspiring, and praising. If you need to get things done through others, you can either get on board with the new, more humane approach or be left in the dust if you refuse to adapt.

Participants in my training programs have shared stories about their leaders telling them their work was shit, they aren't team players, they can't get anything right, and worse. One that's particularly cringe-worthy, yet I've been told some leaders still regularly toss it out in the heat of frustration over a mistake, is that lovely question, "What the hell is wrong with you?" Let's say you're from the old school of management and you think it's perfectly fine to speak to people you lead in this manner. I may not be able to convince you that it's not okay, but you must know that it's not effective. Treating people so disrespectfully does not motivate them to do what you ask or to improve. Acknowledging people's strengths and contributions frequently, explaining to them exactly what you need and why, and thanking people when they do a great job will gain you much greater compliance and loyalty.

With my students at the university, I do all I can to show them that I don't think I'm any smarter or better than they are. I may have more formal education about communication and have more years of experience in the work world, but my students have taught me as much as I've taught them over the years. They know more than I do about countless subjects and I'm always an eager and excited student when someone wants to teach me something new, even if that person is twenty or thirty years younger than I am. As I pointed out in chapter five when I discussed the unique talents and abilities that are identified by an individual's True Colors®, each of us has areas that we could strengthen. We must be open to any potential teachers who can help us grow, regardless of differences in status or rank.

Being a mentor is one of the most important roles one can play in another person's life. I find that people often misuse the term, applying it to relationships that are too casual or lack the impact necessary to make them truly deserving of this title. A mentor is a person who knows you extremely well, sometimes better than you know yourself. A mentor is also someone who plays a significant role in your overall development as a person. Mentors provide holistic support and counsel, not just relative to one aspect of your life, but in the interest of helping you to reach your full potential in all areas.

Mentors provide guidance, push their mentees out of their comfort zones, serve as sounding boards, and advocate for their mentees in a variety of ways, often opening up opportunities mentees would be unable to secure on their own. While mentors are typically older or more experienced, this is not always the case. A mentor can be younger yet wiser or may hold a lower level title but have conquered great obstacles to get to that point, allowing for hard-won, inspiring lessons to pass on. One key aspect of the best mentoring relationships is that they are reciprocal. The mentor fully acknowledges that there is as much to gain from being a mentor as there is from being mentored. Those who have served as mentors know what I mean. To achieve this reciprocity, it's critical that the mentor and mentee treat one another as respected, trusted equals who come together for the mutual benefits of this very sacred connection.

2. SET CLEAR EXPECTATIONS

Be honest now... have you ever gotten angry with someone for not living up to something you expected of him or her and then had to admit that you never clearly articulated that expectation? It's all too easy to do. Recently, one of my students came to me to vent her frustration with another professor. I'll call the student Noreen. I'm often skeptical about these rants, but in this case, the student was one of my best, having proven her dedication to academic excellence on numerous occasions. Noreen reported that she and her group members followed the guidelines for a team presentation exactly as they were outlined on the syllabus. They spent countless hours meeting on campus to make sure every requirement was met. When Noreen challenged the low grade her group received, the professor apparently provided a vague response about how she expected more creativity. When Noreen pointed out that her group met or exceeded every one of the assignment requirements on the syllabus and that there was no mention there of creativity or how that creativity might be demonstrated, the professor became agitated and accused her of challenging her authority. Noreen had no choice but to accept the grade and back off, which seems terribly unfair.

One of the most upsetting experiences my clients seem to be forced to endure as professionals is the dreaded performance review. I have heard endless accounts of the horrors that occur during these meetings. One of the biggest frustrations appears to be that many organizations have performance review systems that make it nearly impossible to earn anything above a satisfactory rating, no matter how much you accomplish. An even bigger insult is when employees are told that they achieved a below satisfactory rating on a dimension that was never clearly identified as an objective in the initial creation of the performance plan. There may have been a general mention of a goal, but it wasn't specific enough for the person to know what the exact target was. This is a setup for failure.

For example, a formerly jubilant and upbeat sales associate who I had worked with in the past came to me looking defeated and depressed. He reported that he received a poor performance review and was on probation because he didn't meet his sales goals for one particular demographic. I asked him what the goal was and how close he came to it. He reported that at the performance planning meeting with his boss at the beginning of the year, the main focus was on increasing sales by 30% for an entirely different demographic so he put most of his energy into that, achieving a stellar 38% increase. There was only a brief mention of also trying to improve sales with the other group, but no specific percentage was identified as a goal, so when the statistics showed that sales only increased by 13% for that group, his overall yearly achievements were viewed as a failure.

3. SET AND COACH OTHERS TO SET SMART GOALS

I know most people have heard of the SMART model for goal setting, but many don't do a very good job of putting it into practice. Goals for yourself and goals you help others set need to be specific, which is what the S in the acronym stands for. Let's use weight loss as an example. You can't just say you want to lose some weight in the next three months. You have to be willing to commit to working to lose an exact number of pounds by a certain date. I will lose ten pounds in the next three months is a great specific goal. It also meets the criterion of being measurable, as represented by the M in the acronym. You just need to get on that old bathroom scale in three months to measure your results.

The A reminds us that goals need to be achievable. Ten pounds in three months is doable for most of us, but you'd have to decide what's realistic for you. The R is for relevant, meaning that the goal has to be aligned with other goals and plans in your life. If you want to get pregnant, it might not be the best time to lose weight. If you're about to go on a cruise, the weight-loss goal might have to wait until you return home so you won't be tortured by the temptation of those spectacular midnight buffets every night for two weeks!

The T is for time-bound, of course. We've already addressed that in our example by making the goal to lose ten pounds in three months. This can be the scariest part for people to commit to. I understand why. If I say I'm going to lose ten pounds in three months and when I get to the deadline, I've only lost seven, I may feel like a failure. But if it were actually me, I wouldn't feel like a failure at all. I would feel like a huge success and you should too if it's you. You lost seven pounds, damn it! That's amazing! Expecting perfection in achieving all our goals isn't realistic, but not setting SMART goals makes progress even less likely. Setting the date would push you harder to work to lose weight than if you had no deadline. So whether you lose the exact amount by the deadline or any weight at all, you're ahead of the game because you practiced SMART goal setting. It's your job to model this approach and coach the people you lead to put it into practice as well.

4. DELIVER CRITICISM CAREFULLY

Providing feedback for improvement is one of the job requirements for any leader, but it must be offered as a gift, which requires emotional intelligence and compassion. The message should be received as something that's meant to be helpful, not hurtful or demeaning. This is one of the hardest parts of being in a leadership position. But just because it's difficult, does not mean we should avoid it. How can the people we coach learn and grow and improve if we don't help them see their blind spots and areas that need work?

I've come across many different models for providing "developmental feedback" in the training programs I've presented in the business world over the years. They may have different acronyms and pretty graphics containing circles and arrows or other attempts to make them seem unique, but they all boil down to the same principles. Step one is to identify the situation you're referring to, in step two you explain the action the person took, step three reveals the negative consequences of that action and step four provides an alternative choice.

Step one is important because if you don't include it, the person on the receiving end of the feedback could be confused about when and where the event occurred. Let's say I need to speak to a student about an inappropriate comment he made in my intercultural communication class. I might ask him to stop by during my office hours and after making friendly small talk for a few minutes, I would dive into the main reason I invited him to see me: "Joe, I wanted to talk with you about the comment you made in class on Tuesday, when we were talking about immigrants in the United States."

Step two can be tough because you have to push yourself to be specific and direct, even if you fear it will be hard for the person to hear. Don't beat around the bush and don't soften your words in this step, otherwise you risk going through this difficult process for no reason because you've sugar coated the message so much that it's completely lost. I would remind Joe of exactly what he said: "When you made the comment that immigrants come to the United States to cheat the welfare system, steal our jobs, and force their weird cultural ways on us..." Yes, believe it or not, students have expressed this opinion and much worse over the years in my classes, which I think should obligate the university to increase my pay to cover the frequent coloring of my prematurely gray head of hair.

For the third step, it's very important that you can identify tangible negative results, not just your opinion about what happened or your speculation about others' reactions. I would need to be able to show Joe the impact of his words in concrete terms, such as: "I could see how upset some of your classmates were by the looks on their faces. Three students also came to see me after class to express how offended they were because they themselves are hard-working, tax-paying immigrants, who have come to the United States for a better life and to contribute all that they can to our country."

I find that step four is commonly skipped, which is extremely problematic. How many times has someone criticized you but given you no clue as to what you could do to correct the situation or do better next time? If you're going to tell people that you're not happy with something they did or said, you MUST also tell them what they could do or say differently that would make you happy, or at least keep you neutral. To minimize damage to self-esteem and maintain positive relationships, I often try to add something positive to this step, if I can do so genuinely. But that's optional and works in some situations and not others.

I might say to Joe, "I know you're a good guy and you didn't mean to hurt anyone's feelings. You have a lot of friends in class and I'm sure they're willing to overlook this one instance as long as it doesn't happen again. In the future, please take a breath and think before you speak in class. Consider if the way you're planning to say something could be perceived as an attack on or generalization about a particular group. It's also helpful to use 'I' language, speaking for yourself, what you think, your concerns, and the reasons you have those concerns." I might even give Joe specific language for times when he wanted to express similar thoughts on the issue: "Personally, I feel worried that immigrants will take the scarce resources and jobs we have for people in our country. I just want to take care of our own citizens and I don't know how we can do that if we keep letting so many immigrants in."

Sometimes we're generally happy with someone's work and only need to make one small suggestion for improvement. In these cases, and in similar situations with anyone in your life, I recommend replacing the word "but" with "and" anytime you can to lessen the weight of your feedback. For example, a student recently came to me to find out why she received a low A on her paper instead of a high A. I said something along the lines of, "Your research was excellent and you drew some interesting conclusions about the topic. You did a very good job and next time, just make sure to proofread very carefully so I don't have to take off points for small typos." Try replacing "and next time" with "but next time" to see the difference. Believe it or not, though it's only three letters, the "but" in comments such as this one have been shown to stir significantly higher defensiveness and hurt feelings.

One of my favorite books on management — an oldie, but a real goodie — is *The One Minute Manager*. I still assign it as required reading for my organizational communication class and even generation Y students tend to love it and find it relevant and applicable in their work lives. You really should read it, and to entice you I'll just say that the suggestions on giving feedback for improvement in the book reinforce and elaborate on what I've shared here in ways that have profoundly impacted and improved my leadership style. The tips on goal setting and providing praise are great too.

5. BE GENEROUS WITH PRAISE

I mentioned this in the chapter on communicating with your boss, but it bears repeating here: many studies show that appreciation is one of the top motivators for people to repeat and improve high performance. Positive reinforcement keeps people wanting to do well and pushes them to do better. I have had debates with managers on this issue many times. They will suggest that giving too much praise makes people lazy. They worry that if they tell their employees how well they're doing all the time, they'll have little incentive to do better. I understand this thinking, but it is totally unsupported by psychological research. Praise and appreciation are like a drug: when you get some, you want to keep getting it and you want to get more. Most people who receive regular appreciation for their efforts will be highly motivated to keep doing a great job and will feel compelled to keep improving so that they can enjoy more yummy approval. We all love it, whether we're willing to admit it or not.

Another question that often arises when I discuss praise in training programs is whether we should only acknowledge efforts that go above and beyond expectations or to also occasionally mention our appreciation when people simply do what they're supposed to do. I think we should do both. For example, my husband is also one of my greatest mentors. His appreciation for the things I do means a lot to me. When our kids were babies, he would thank me for things like breastfeeding them, doing their laundry, and reading to them. Those activities were nothing exceptional and most people view them as the standard obligations of one who chooses to have a child. But being a mother can be a thankless, exhausting job, so a little recognition goes a long way.

The general recommendations for providing praise are similar to those that I shared above with regard to delivering feedback for improvement. You can follow the same model, except for the fourth step, because it's not necessary. Telling someone they did well and making them feel great is one of my favorite things to do. Studies show that making someone's day is a win-win for all involved. It's not only great for the receiver. The giver can experience the high of how good it feels to boost someone else's self-esteem and make their day. There's also often a ripple effect because that person then passes on their positivity and good feelings to others in his or her life.

In one of my classes this past semester, I used a new textbook and gave a particularly challenging midterm exam. The questions came mostly from the test bank for the book. I thought the students were well prepared for it because they were so engaged in class when we discussed all the concepts and theories. I was disappointed to discover that the overall grade range was significantly lower than it usually is in my classes. I analyzed the test, the questions, and tried to figure out what went wrong. After realizing that some questions could have been misleading and some multiple-choice options too similar, I decided to curve the grades.

Even after my adjustments, only two students out of forty-eight earned a score of 100%. I sat for a minute picturing those two young women in my mind. They were both always in class and never late, participated with enthusiasm, and had turned in outstanding essays. To be honest, I also really liked each of them because they had been kind and friendly to me and expressed gratitude for my approach to teaching. I was about to move on to the next task when I remembered how much I push leaders to take every opportunity to provide praise. So I sent each of my two students a quick email letting them know that they were one of only two students to earn 100% on the test. I told them what drive their grade demonstrated, and that serious students like them keep me motivated to up my game as a teacher. It took a couple of minutes at most. Later that day, I received responses from both of them thanking me for my message. They each said it made their entire weekend, since I had sent the email on a Saturday morning. Ahhh, that felt so good and it was so easy.

Anytime you find yourself thinking about how much you appreciate what someone else did or said, whether it was something small or large, make it a point to tell the person. Make it specific and share what the outcome was. I'll show you how it's done by thanking you, yes you. I want to thank you for buying and reading my book. As I was writing it, I had doubts about whether anyone would be interested in a book on communication skills. Every reader makes a difference for me and helps me to feel more confident in believing that I have something of value to share. So I thank you, sincerely.

6. BONUS FUN TIP: BE THE "COOL" BOSS OR TEACHER AND ENJOY DOING IT

I was recently preparing to deliver a workshop on increasing influencing skills for Google. I was thrilled to find that studies by influence expert, Dr. Terry Bacon, show that "likability" is one of the most powerful factors in our ability to influence others. Bacon explores this and other important aspects of the powers of influence in his books, such as *Elements of Influence*, which I got a lot out of. How could anyone deny that we are more likely to listen to, work hard for, want to impress, and be supportive of a leader who we like, admire, and enjoy being with?

I am not suggesting that you shirk your responsibility of holding people to high standards. I do believe, though, that you can demand stellar performance while also being friendly, approachable, easy-going, and even silly at times. I love it when I make some kind of joke while teaching and get a big laugh. It's especially fun when my humor is self-deprecating, showing that I don't take myself too seriously and am well aware that we all make mistakes and have our embarrassing moments. I've been told that my honesty about my flaws and willingness to poke fun at myself helps others to open up and feel comfortable with me, whether they are students or clients.

I believe the leaders who are most influential and have the greatest potential of being true mentors are the ones who aren't afraid to reveal themselves and forge deep and sincere connections with others. They are the people who know how to strike just the right balance between being warm and accessible while also inspiring people to consistently do their best.

The Bottom Line:

1. Regardless of status, treat everyone with the same respect you expect.
2. Communicate goals, instructions, and explanations as clearly as possible.
3. Model and teach how to set and achieve goals.
4. Provide feedback for improvement with sensitivity and empathy.
5. Bolster motivation with appreciation for both big wins and daily deliverables.
6. Be likable, pleasant, fun, and generous. Don't take yourself too seriously.

CHAPTER 9

COMMUNICATING WITH YOUR FRIENDS

1. BE A GOOD LISTENER

Being a good friend means being a good listener. With our increasing use of technology to communicate, it has become more challenging to listen attentively in face-to-face interactions. True listening is very rare. True listening means that you maintain eye contact, resisting the temptation to check your phone for messages. True listening means that you are facing the person you're listening to, are engaged, nodding, and using following sounds such as "uh-huh" to show that you're fully present. True listening means that you give the other person plenty of time to speak without interrupting, turning the conversation back to you, or one-upping your friend's story or situation by saying something along the lines of, "You think that's bad, wait till you hear what happened to me..."

When I overhear people's conversations, I don't hear a lot of good listening going on. Maybe this is why I'm often asked to address listening skills in my communication training programs. To make my top recommendations easy to remember, I came up with an acronym. If you reread the paragraph above, I bet you can guess what it is. TRUE listening stands for: Tune in, Read all signs, Understand, and Empathize. If you practice TRUE listening with your friends and others in your life, you will be giving them a beautiful gift.

Tuning in means tuning out distractions. It requires setting aside all technology, as I mentioned above. But it also means turning off the chatter in your own mind, which is often self-focused and pointless, to be blunt. Get out of the prison of your own head and give your full attention to your friend. The people you care about need you to listen actively and focus on what they're experiencing, feeling, thinking, and struggling with, without having your attention repeatedly drawn to unimportant sights, sounds, and internal thoughts.

Reading all signs means that you work to pay attention to nonverbal cues as well as the words that are being spoken. Is your friend telling you that she's just fine even though you notice a sad, heavy expression on her face or her tone of voice is unconvincing? There have been times when I was suffering over something yet didn't say anything to the friend I was with, and other times it came pouring out even though I hadn't planned for it to. Sometimes I just don't know how to express what I'm feeling so I hold it in. This is not good, I know, but I'm human. Looking back, I can see that what usually makes all the difference in whether I disclose my true feelings or not is how easy it is to get the person to accept my false claim that everything is great. Certain people I know are too perceptive, caring, and too tuned in to me to let me get away with hiding what's really going on. But most people are not.

Understanding your friend as you listen means that you work hard to try to see things from that person's point of view, given what you know about your friend's life experiences, beliefs, fears and insecurities, etc. It's important to fight the natural tendency to filter everything through your own perspectives and biases. You can understand without agreeing. You can understand without having had the same experience, though that is not the same as feeling what your friend has felt.

If you get to the point of being the kind of listener who can Tune in, Read all signs, and Understand, you're ready for the final step of TRUE listening: Empathy. While understanding occurs on the inside, empathy is expressed. Even though "Understand" is part of my acronym, it's not always the best word to use when expressing empathy, unless you've gone through the exact same situation.

For example, I have a friend who lost a child. I cannot begin to imagine how that would feel. I have tried hard to understand, but I can only do that to a certain extent. If my friend were to share how she's feeling and what she plans to do on the anniversary of the day her daughter passed away, a response that includes the words, "I understand" would probably not be a good choice. How could I possibly understand? Instead, I might say, "I can't even imagine how you're feeling. It must be so hard to get through this day every year. It makes perfect sense that you want to spend it alone looking at pictures and remembering her." That's empathy. It doesn't suggest full understanding or that you've gone through the same thing or had the same feelings. It's just an expression of your acknowledgement of what the person is feeling, why he or she is feeling it, and what the person has chosen to do about it, with full acceptance and validation.

You can demonstrate empathy even when you don't see things the same way. Let's say a friend of mine is angry with her husband over something that wouldn't bother me. I can still empathize with a response such as, "I can see why you would feel that way, given what you've been through in your marriage and the things that have happened in the past."

2. WORK TOWARD A RELATIVE DEGREE OF RECIPROCITY

If you want to have close, enduring, and rewarding friendships, it's important that you don't make everything all about you. In fact, this is essential in all of your relationships. Some people dominate conversations, thinking that what they have to say and what they're going through is much more important than what anyone else might have to share. Some people expect their friends to listen to their problems and worries for hours and don't reciprocate by asking about how others are doing. If you think you might be this type of person, it's time to change your ways.

One of my favorite quotes comes from a great book called *How to Win Friends and Influence People* by Dale Carnegie: "You can make more friends in two months by becoming interested in other people than you can in two years by trying to get other people interested in you." People who think too highly of themselves and don't show that they genuinely care about others' lives and interests do not make good friends. Please honestly assess the possibility that you don't let others get a word in edgewise during discussions or that you think your issues are more important than other people's. If this is a problem for you, stop yourself when you realize you've been talking for a while and ask questions. Then follow the advice in the first recommendation of this chapter: be a good listener!

Dominating conversations and making things all about you is not the only concern when considering whether or not friendships are reciprocal. It's also about the give-and-take healthy friendships tend to involve. I'm not saying that every time you do a favor for a friend, you should expect a favor in return. That would actually be quite selfish. Let's say Joanne and Maria have been friends for years when Maria starts to realize that she is constantly doing things for Joanne, spending hours listening to her problems, helping her with projects, etc. Maria also realizes that Joanne never seems available when she needs help with something and always turns the discussion back to herself if Maria opens up about something she's upset or excited about. How good would you feel about your friendship with Joanne if you were Maria? I'm not suggesting that we should feel obligated to do things for our friends just because they do things for us. Instead, I think we should want to do things for them because we love and appreciate them and it makes us happy to help them.

3. ACCEPT YOUR FRIENDS AS THEY ARE

When I realized that I didn't have the power to change my friends, I started enjoying them so much more. I couldn't make the friend who hasn't found a life partner yet take on more hobbies that might help her meet people. I couldn't convince the friend who has the opposite political views as me to see how wrong she is (please read that with sarcasm). I couldn't get the friend who's unhappy with her weight to stick to the eating plan I shared with her. So, rather than continue to beat my head against a brick wall, I decided to love and accept my friends as they are.

Albert Einstein said that insanity is doing the same thing over and over and expecting a different result. I know he was really smart, but I have to disagree with him on this. I think doing the same thing over and over and expecting a different result is something we all do regularly, in various areas of our lives, for as long as we live. If we can accept this fact with more grace and compassion, we will free ourselves of a great deal of stress, worry, and planning that serves no purpose.

It can be very difficult to watch your friends do self-destructive things. But the reality is that most of us have our own unhealthy vices and most of us make choices that aren't the best for us at times. It is often the friends who know and care about us most who can clearly see that we are hurting ourselves, whether it involves staying in a relationship that's not working or smoking cigarettes. What I've learned is that planning confrontations, judging, or making passive aggressive comments does not help things.

You don't necessarily have to hide your feelings. If the subject comes up, you can lovingly express your views. For example, I might have a friend who says to me, "I know smoking is so bad for me, and I really want to quit." That would be an opportunity for me to respond with something such as, "Yeah, I know how hard it is to quit. I used to smoke a long time ago and I tried a lot of different ways to stop before one finally worked. It would be great if you could find a way too. What do you think might work for you?"

When I say accept your friends as they are, I don't mean that you should not encourage them to improve their lives and make changes that would benefit them. I've just found that the best time to provide this kind of support is when a person expresses the desire to change. Self-improvement efforts are often short lived if they're only in the interest of pleasing or avoiding the judgment of others.

Another part of accepting your friends as they are means that you are open to discussing and learning from the differences between you. It's important that we have friends whose lives and beliefs are similar to and different from our own. If all your friends are just like you, you're missing out. I've had friends who have kids say that people who aren't parents themselves have no business giving child-rearing advice. I don't think this is true and have gotten some very high quality input on issues with my kids from friends who are not parents. Everyone had parents or caregivers of some kind, so doesn't that earn them the right to a perspective on the subject? I think so. I also remember complaining about some frustration with my husband to a friend (which I rarely do, really!) who happened to be single. She was empathetic, but said something about how it seemed like a small issue compared to how great he is and that it was hard for her to understand, because she would love to be with someone as supportive and reliable as my husband is. It shifted my feelings in an instant and I appreciated her honesty.

4. HELP GENERATE OPTIONS RATHER THAN GIVING ADVICE

I can't even tell you how many times I've gotten into big trouble by responding too honestly to a question that started with, "I want to get your advice on something." I know friends have said that to you, and I know they will say it to you again in the future. Here's my interpretation of what they often really mean: "I want to get a frustrating situation off my chest. I just want to talk about it for a while with someone who's a good listener and won't judge me." If you're one of those people who likes to try to fix all your friends' problems, let me tell you what they're probably too afraid to say: "Stop trying to fix me! I

116

know what I should do, damn it. But I don't want to or I'm not ready to, or maybe I even need to hit rock bottom before I'm willing to."

So, what should you do when you're asked for advice? Please see tip number one. Be a good listener. Ask good questions, not confrontational questions, but questions that encourage your friend to dig deeper, to see things in a new light. For example, I was recently talking to a friend who is having an affair with a married man. It is not my place to judge or make her feel worse about the situation. But I am concerned about her well-being as well as that of all who are involved, including the wife and children of this man, even though I don't know them. Some questions I might consider asking her are: "Where do you see this going?" "How are you going to manage the guilt you just described?" and, "What qualities do you love about him that you could look for in someone who's available for a relationship?"

I feel that it would be a mistake for me to give my friend advice in this particular situation. If I said something such as, "You need to end this right now. You deserve better and you're going to feel horrible if you destroy his family," she would not feel safe opening up to me again. In addition to that, she would not be any more likely to end the affair. Telling people what to do in a self-righteous, holier-than-thou manner rarely does any good, unless what you want is to create distance in the friendship.

When someone needs counsel and support, try approaches such as, "What are your choices in this situation?" "What are some of the ways you could respond to him?" or, "How could you tell her how you feel?" If your friend identifies three different options and you want to scream because you believe that one is clearly "the right one," I would urge you to hold back. If you truly want to help, don't reveal your preference too soon. Instead, ask your friend to walk through the pros and cons of each choice and if you're right (which you may not be, sorry), the truth shall set you both free.

5. BE THERE FOR THEM AT THE IMPORTANT TIMES

The father of one of my closest and oldest friends from college passed away not long ago. He was a wonderful, funny, generous man who was always kind to our group of friends as well as all of our children. My friend planned a service to celebrate his life at her home and of course, my husband and kids and I went. But I also decided to drive separately so that I could stay later than everyone else to help clean up. I could tell you that I did this because this particular friend has been such a loyal and supportive friend to me over the years and I wanted to reciprocate and that would be true. But really, I just wanted to be there for her because I love her so much and knew how much pain she must be in. Washing dishes and hanging around later was not a big thing at all. It was a small thing, but it was on an important day, a day I have yet to experience, but that I imagine will always be remembered, along with the people who were there to grieve with me and help me.

It's tough to admit this, but I haven't always made the right choices in this area. I have missed important dates for friends or neglected to check in on them when I knew I should. Two situations in particular stand out in my mind and though they were both a long time ago, I still regret them and feel guilty about them. But I see this guilt as a good thing, thanks to what I've learned from Dr. Brené Brown. She's a renowned psychologist who researches and writes about shame. Her book, *The Gifts of*

Imperfection, released me from a great deal of the shame I had been carrying around. She explains that shame is harmful to us, while guilt doesn't have to be. Feeling a little guilty about a choice you made that didn't live up to what you expect of yourself may compel you to do better next time. That doesn't mean you should beat yourself up over it though. Feeling shame is much worse.

Let's say you don't call your friend back for two days even though she left you a message saying she really needed to talk. Feeling shame would sound like this: "I'm a horrible friend. I don't deserve to have the good friends that I have. I can't even get it together enough to be there for people who need me." That kind of thinking is likely to make things worse. If you feel that bad about letting two days pass before calling your friend back, you may never bring yourself to call. Instead, you might tell yourself, "Damn, I really should have called back sooner. I want to be the kind of friend who's there for people. I'm feeling kind of guilty about this and want to do better." A reasonable degree of guilt that nudges you to do better is healthy. Wallowing in shame is not — it does nothing good for you or your friends.

6. BONUS FUN TIP: PLAN A YEARLY GETAWAY WITH FRIENDS YOU LOVE

Three of my most favorite, fun girlfriends and I just celebrated our ten-year anniversary together. We've been friends for much longer than that, but the anniversary was an acknowledgement that despite often living in different parts of the country, the birth of children, and a variety of other life-changing events, we have gotten together for a night away at least once every year. These ladies are the kind of friends who I can totally be myself with and I cannot begin to express to you what

119

those getaways mean to me and do for me. They bring me back to life. They remind me of who I really am and what I really want.

What do we do together that has such a magical effect on me? I hope my friends forgive me for revealing the following because some people reading this will know who they are. Still, I have to tell you our secrets in case it gives you permission to do whatever your silly things with your friends are. We eat and drink too much. We usually make a scene by laughing way too loud and daring each other to do embarrassing things. We dance and sing songs to each other in our hotel room. Some of the dances we've come up with are quite ridiculous but we love them. We keep an ongoing Google document of the funny things that are said on these getaways. One time in Las Vegas, I accidentally typed "Vefas" in a text message to one of these pals, so Vegas will forever be Vefas to the four of us now. I wonder what people think when they see our regular mentions of trips to Vefas on social media, but I don't really care.

Despite the crazy antics that occur on our yearly getaways, there is never any shortage of conversation about what's going on in all our lives, what we're having a hard time with, and how important our friendship is to us. Sometimes I'm truly astounded by how much we can pack into twenty-four hours, but we do it, and our lives are so, so much richer for it. Love you ladies!

The Bottom Line:

1. Be the best friend you can be by practicing true active listening.
2. Make sure there's give and take. Don't be selfish.
3. Accept and love your friends wherever they are on their journey.
4. Minimize giving advice. Help your friends help themselves.
5. Be there for your friends when they need you, whether they ask or not.
6. Enjoy regular fun time with the friends you love and can be yourself with.

CHAPTER 10

COMMUNICATING THROUGH TECHNOLOGY

1. COMMUNICATE CLEARLY, CONCISELY, AND CONVERSATIONALLY

I'm always trying to find ways to help people remember my top tips, so acronyms and alliteration are great friends. I was pretty excited when I came up with the three Cs. They fit into almost any training program I'm delivering, especially when I talk about professional communication. Being concise may not always be so important in interpersonal conversations, but being clear and conversational will almost always be your best bet.

When you're communicating through some form of technology, make sure that your message is crystal clear. It's worth it to invest extra time in crafting your message so that you don't have to spend time dealing with misunderstandings and questions about what you meant later. Don't waste people's time by making them read that email or text message over and over to figure out what you're trying to say.

It's also problematic if your tone is unclear. Are you angry? Excited? Neutral? I've heard way too many stories about people misinterpreting the tone of some type of virtual message. How can we avoid this? Read your words several times before sending them. Consider the receiver. Think about how what you've written might be misconstrued and change the wording to eliminate that possibility. If you think there's any chance of something coming across as harsh or confrontational and it's not meant to be, CHANGE IT!

I also happen to like using emoticons to convey the tone of a message. I know some people don't, but I've been surprised by the increase in their use by many people I work with, even high-level corporate types. I appreciate seeing a smiley face at the end of an email request or getting a wink along with a sarcastic comment sent through a social media site. To play it safe, I recommend avoiding the use of emoticons in your professional communication unless the other person uses them first.

Being concise requires that you say what you need to say in as few words as possible and use small, simple words. When you notice that your message is getting lengthy and you know deep down that it doesn't really need to be, delete the whole thing and start over. Force yourself to stick to only the most important facts and details. Don't unnecessarily suck up the precious and limited minutes of someone's day with extra or irrelevant information. Don't you appreciate it when others are concise with their virtual requests and responses, allowing you to move on to the rest of your tasks quickly?

Some people fight me on my preferences for brevity by saying that their boss or some other person they communicate with regularly wants lots of detail. Fine, always adapt to the other person's preferences in whatever ways you're comfortable doing so. But know that I hear far more complaints about messages that are too verbose than those that are too brief. When in doubt, you can always ask questions to find out which way to go. If you have piles of research you could potentially present, before dumping it all into an online report that would take an hour to read, simply inquire: "Did you want me to give you a detailed rundown of what I've found or just a few bullet points on my key findings?"

When I started out in the business world a couple of decades ago, some communication was still pretty formal. I remember addressing letters with "Dear Sir" or writing, "As per our conversation" in a fax cover letter. Thankfully, professional communication has become much more relaxed and straightforward. Though some people my age lament the changes, I say we need to be flexible and go with the flow. Many of the clients I work with are much younger than I am and I learn a lot from them about how to adapt to new generations.

One young program manager I work with regularly recently apologized for not responding to my email by saying, "I don't really do email anymore. Just text me when you need something." No problem for me! She responds right away when I text and it's easy enough to do. Another client starts all her emails to me with, "Hey Bridget," and engages in very informal chatter in messages, which I love. She's also in London, which debunks the stereotype that British people are stuffy. Conversational communication is extremely important when we communicate through technology because it can be a cold, impersonal medium. We must do all we can to convey a friendly, upbeat tone and create strong connections with people even if face-to-face communication is not an option.

In my Mastering Business Communication course, I provide a before and after example of a message to prove that we'd all prefer the more clear, concise, and conversational version. Imagine the following as an email or voicemail message: "Marshall asked me to convey his deep regret for the fact that the meeting was held at a time when he could not be available due to his longstanding prior commitment related to an important speaking engagement at the annual charity function organized by our corporate headquarters."

A person should only have to read a message once to fully understand it. How many times would it take you to read the last sentence of the previous paragraph to grasp it? Chances are that even after reading it four of five times you'd still have a number of questions about what the heck this person is trying to say! It's totally unclear. Why couldn't Marshall go to the meeting? Does he regret that he couldn't attend or that the meeting was held at a time when he wasn't available? I could ask many more questions that would be impossible to answer, given this vague, wordy approach.

Here's the alternative: "Marshall asked me to let you know that he's very sorry he had to miss the meeting. He was giving the keynote address at our annual charity function." Short and sweet. Clear, concise, and conversational.

2. PROOFREAD YOUR WRITING, EVEN IN TEXTS AND EMAILS

I am fascinated by the regular rants that I come across about poorly written emails, texts, blog posts, reports, tweets, Facebook posts, etc. Why is it that just because we're saying something through some type of technology, some of us feel there's less need to make sure that it's written clearly and properly? This makes no sense to me, given how much of our communication takes place through these channels.

You create a powerful impression of yourself through your written communication online. Many people are sticklers for correct grammar, punctuation, and spelling. It's not that difficult to take a moment to make sure your writing is error free. If you didn't learn the basics well back in elementary school or have forgotten the rules, it's time for a refresher. Bookmark one of the many grammar sites on the Internet. I visit them regularly when I'm writing. I'm sorry to be the bearer of bad news, but if "they're" is spelled "there" or the apostrophe in the word "parent's" isn't in the right place, you will be judged. I've asked professionals in my workshops to share their perceptions of people who make a lot of mistakes in their writing and some of the most common responses are: lazy, lacking intelligence, careless, and uneducated.

If you don't care about these things, know that you are in the minority. Most people do care and are annoyed by the butchering of their language and the way it's meant to be written. It's worth your time to make sure your email communication, blog posts and comments, tweets, and so on are clearly worded and thoroughly proofread.

I realize that I run the risk of someone finding a mistake or two in this book and calling me a hypocrite for making this point with such force. But I am not talking about a mistake or two. That would be entirely forgivable, especially in a lengthy work. I have found small mistakes in almost every textbook I've used in my classes and most novels I've read. As long as the content is valuable, this is not a big problem. But when we communicate through technology, our messages tend to be relatively brief, causing each error to stand out and diminish the author's credibility.

3. BE CAUTIOUS ABOUT WHAT YOU REVEAL

My younger son recently told me an interesting story about a website he visits regularly. He said people post rants and crazy opinions that he finds entertaining. Thankfully, he doesn't actually engage with these people in any way. Apparently, this one kid was getting on everyone's nerves for some reason. All the kid had to do was post a picture of himself and the front of his house and from that limited information, someone was able to figure out exactly where he lived. I was relieved to learn that whoever figured it out was not interested in harming the kid, at least not physically. Still, it must have been quite an inconvenience to deal with the delivery of thirty pizzas that he didn't order.

I'm sure you've heard the accounts of people falling in love online only to find out that behind the picture of the stunning supermodel look-alike was an obese seventy-year-old pedophile. But are you one of those people who don't think something like that could happen to you? Kidnappings, burglaries, identity theft, and worse have occurred because people were not careful about the personal information they shared online.

In addition to protecting yourself by not revealing personal information online or through other forms of technology, please, don't post embarrassing information or photographs of yourself. If you wouldn't want your boss, your professor, your mother, your neighbor, or the person you hope to date to see it, do not post it online. I have stumbled upon everything from naked pictures of my students to barely decipherable posts by inebriated colleagues, all of which I would rather not have been exposed to, as magnanimous as I strive to be. I was especially horrified to find one of the most vicious homophobic Facebook diatribes I've ever seen, by someone I formerly thought highly of. The majority of employers search the Internet for the "truth" about potential employees. Drunken photographs, profanity in posts, and highly personal revelations have resulted in the choice not to hire someone and in some cases, have provided grounds for firing.

I've had many debates with people about whether or not I should be Facebook friends with my students. Some of my colleagues keep their personal lives private and do not engage with students through any form of social media. I completely understand their reasoning and respect their choice. I have a different take on this issue though. I am happy to connect with my students on Facebook because I don't post anything that I wouldn't be comfortable with anyone in my life seeing. I like to post inspiring messages, pictures of my family and pets, and to engage with others about interesting ideas and events. If I were going to post something on my Facebook timeline that I wouldn't want my students to see, then it probably wouldn't be appropriate to post in general. I've also found social media a great way to stay in touch with students who I've bonded with or to get a better understanding of what current students may be struggling with and how I can help.

I am often surprised by how easy it is to find people's information and pictures online even when those people think their privacy settings would only allow their friends to have access. Make no mistake about this: anything you put out into cyberspace can be found and shared by anyone. I cannot emphasize enough that it's not worth the risk. Keep your pictures and messages clean. I would also recommend keeping them relatively positive. Imagine that you're about to hire a new employee and with a quick Google search, you find your top candidate's blog. As you read it, you discover that the posts are extremely hostile and put a negative spin on every topic that's addressed. Would it influence your decision about hiring this person?

4. DON'T SAY ANYTHING YOU WOULDN'T SAY TO SOMEONE IN PERSON

People reveal things to others online that they would never have the courage to say to their faces. This is as true for cruel comments about others as it is about declarations of love. We have all heard the stories of bullies who publicly post terrible things about or nude pictures of the people they want to hurt. Please don't be part of this nastiness, in any way, and when you see it, report it or fight against it any way you can. This kind of attack has ruined lives, sometimes even resulting in suicide. If you're not familiar with the story of Amanda Todd, I encourage you to search for it on YouTube and imagine how you would feel if you went through what she had to endure.

If you want to ask someone on a date or say "I love you" to your partner for the first time, please have the courage to do it face-to-face. While I think all the communication technology we have available to use can bring us closer, it can also be used to hide behind. Studies in interpersonal communication are beginning to show that people are much braver with what they're willing to say through communication technology than what they will express in person. This concerns me and I hope it concerns you too.

One of my favorite quotes about this issue comes from Edward R. Murrow: "The newest computer can merely compound, at speed, the oldest problem in the relations between human beings, and in the end the communicator will be confronted with the old problem, of what to say and how to say it." Your choice of words is just as important when you send them through some form of technology as it is when you're looking into someone's eyes as you're speaking.

Here's a good rule to follow… anytime you're experiencing some degree of anxiety about something you want to communicate… do it in person. You wouldn't send a marriage proposal in a text, email, or tweet, would you? Neither should you give developmental feedback to an employee, confront a friend about an issue you've been avoiding, or publicly debate a controversial political issue with a family member by hiding behind technology.

My final word on this subject comes from a place of deep regret. I have had "text arguments" with my husband that I forced myself to read later, once the issue had been resolved. To my horror, my words were insensitive, inflammatory, and grossly exaggerated the situation. But I could not take them back. Yes, I have asked my husband to delete those messages and I have deleted them myself. But just as we are drawn to rubberneck at the car wreck on the freeway, I have reread my awful messages multiple times and I fear he may have too, simply because they were there, burned into that damn little screen that has way too much power over so many of our lives. I beg you not to engage in arguments with loved ones through text messaging. Chances are that you won't want a written record of the things you've said and they'll be much easier for your victim to forget if they can't be reviewed over and over.

5. DEVELOP AND MAINTAIN GENUINE CONNECTIONS WITH PEOPLE

Now that I've gotten my words of caution out of the way, let me take things in a different direction. I think that communicating through technology can be a beautiful way to develop and maintain genuine and intimate connections with others.

As a working wife and mother who enjoys keeping busy with projects I'm passionate about, I can't always find the time to connect in person with all of the people I'd like to see. I'm well aware that instant messaging someone on Facebook or retweeting their tweet on Twitter can't compare to chatting across a dinner table but they are better than nothing, aren't they? I have found many satisfying ways to use social media to stay connected to the people I care about.

I have about eighty cousins spread out all over the United States. Thanks to Facebook, I can see pictures of them and their kids, be reminded to send loving birthday messages, and get a sense of what's going on in their lives. Because I travel for work frequently, I use social media to send group messages letting family and friends know when I'll be in their neck of the woods. This has resulted in many wonderful get-togethers that I might not have taken the time to set up if multiple time-consuming phone calls were required. I also love staying in touch with friends from my youth. Having moved across the country at fourteen years old, I was sad to lose touch with many of my old pals. Finding them and being able to catch up so many years later, due to the genius of Mark Zuckerberg, has been a true blessing.

I've been a part of many helpful online discussion groups — for authors, for parents, etc. Conversations that begin in a large group often branch off into continued discussion in smaller groups, sometimes between just two of us. After engaging in a few ongoing personal conversations that felt genuinely intimate, I became curious about whether the rapport developed online would translate into face-to-face interactions. So I started to test it.

I have now had in-person meetings with three women who I initially became friends with online. This is another perk of traveling for business, because all three of them live in different parts of the country. In each case, the relationship we built through technology proved to be a solid foundation for spending hours together having a great time and communicating just as comfortably and openly as we had over the Internet. My fond memories of time spent with these three women include strolling the New York City Highline together at sunset, reflecting on life and relationships over a delicious bottle of wine, and staying to talk for hours after finishing our lattes in a Las Vegas Starbucks.

I've recently discovered that we can even create a meaningful learning experience with a large group of people through technology. Not long ago, I facilitated training that was shared all over the world through video conferencing technology for the first time. I was nervous about whether or not I'd be able to joke around, engage people, and generate discussion the way I normally do. To my surprise and delight, I was able to do all this and more. Sure, face-to-face communication would have been better, but it wasn't possible in this case. By taking advantage of the systems my client had in place, I was able to share valuable content with people in Bombay,

Copenhagen, Tokyo, and London all at the same time. I urge you to be open to learning and using the new forms of communication technology that become available to us in the future. Don't be afraid of it and don't resist the inevitable changes. I find it incredibly exciting to think about all the ways we'll be able to connect with others that we can't even fathom in the present moment!

6. BONUS FUN TIP: SAFELY PLAY ONLINE

I know some people who refuse to join Facebook or engage in social media in any way and I can absolutely understand the reasons why. It can take over one's life and create expectations for regular communication with people we wouldn't otherwise want to have anything to do with. I also realize that some people find themselves addicted to social media and waste countless hours posting and reading meaningless nonsense. But, for those of us who don't have these challenges, I think the Internet can be an exciting playground!

I often spend long hours working at my computer. Many studies on productivity say we need regular breaks to recharge our batteries. I realize that different methods work for different people, but I believe that almost everyone can find something that works for them in the online world. Sometimes when I finish a writing goal, I'll allow myself fifteen minutes to post something on a social media site and read what's going on with my friends. Other times, when my brain is fried and I need to wake it up, I am shocked by how reenergized I feel after playing a few of my turns in online word games with friends for ten minutes. I'll even admit that when the workday is done, and I feel I've earned a few minutes of pure junk food for the brain, I'll fish around for news on my favorite celebrities. Don't judge, okay, I get a lot done and we all need an escape from time to time.

Maybe you're like my younger son who considers educational websites such as Khan Academy fun to peruse. He is like a walking encyclopedia these days. Or perhaps you've always dreamed of reading the classics but never found the time. Most of them are available to read on your computer or e-reader for a relatively low cost. They also often come in the audiobook version. You might be surprised by how much more confident you feel about the literature category in trivia games with just a fifteen-minute-a-day investment on one of your devices.

I couldn't possibly tell you all the ways you can find to use technology to add more fun and play to your life, but I can assure you there is a way that you would love and it would enrich your life more than you can imagine. But beware of the potential for addiction and limit your playtime so that it doesn't cut into the important things you should be doing. Just like elementary school kids, we all need a recess period during our day!

The Bottom Line:

1. Be clear, concise, and conversational in all your virtual communication.
2. Well-written, well-edited messages are essential regardless of the medium.
3. Don't reveal too much about yourself or post embarrassing material online.
4. Save the important stuff for face-to-face communication.
5. Be open to creating and growing close connections through technology.
6. As long as you're safe and productive, make time to play online.

CONCLUSION

After spending many hours contemplating how to close this book, two paradoxical thoughts keep coming to me: that I am happy with it and ready to give birth to it, and also that there is so much I wanted to say but didn't.

I am happy with this book because I have successfully opened a conversation with you by sharing some of the most important lessons I've learned about how to be an effective communicator. I'm also pleased with the range of topics I was able to address in a short, practical guide. I did my best to be honest and to speak with you as informally as I could, given the limitations of this medium. Finally, I'm confident that most people who read this book will find at least one or two suggestions that, if put into practice, will improve their lives and relationships significantly.

Still, there is far more in my heart, mind, and soul that I desperately want to share with you than what you'll find in the pages contained here. In reflecting on the chapters on leadership and communication with your boss, I would have liked to reveal my thoughts on the differences between being a manager and a leader. When I talked about my marriage and being a mother, my words did not come close to conveying how profoundly these relationships have shaped my views. Similarly, my brief mentions of my spiritual practice may erroneously suggest that this is a small part of my life, when in reality, it is the foundation for everything I believe.

But, I forgive myself for these omissions and I hope you will too, because this is my very first book on communication. I must trust that the ideas that found their way to these pages will be enough of a start to my relationship with you as a reader. I know that the subjects I didn't address or didn't cover as thoroughly as I could have will find their way into future books, articles, blog posts, or maybe even a face-to-face conversation between you and me someday.

There is an acronym floating around the Internet that sums up everything I've said in this book perfectly. I don't know who to attribute it to because I've seen it all over, so forgive me if you're the one who came up with it. The acronym is THINK and it reminds us that before we speak, we should ask ourselves whether or not what we're about to say is True, Helpful, Inspiring, Necessary and Kind. Beautiful guidelines to live by... in my opinion.

My final word is this: when your communication comes from a place of love, compassion, respect, inner peace, celebration of difference, and radical self-acceptance, you will become the person you were meant to be and together we can begin to heal the world.

ACKNOWLEDGEMENTS

I can't imagine who I would be without my family. My parents were my first teachers and oh, the things they taught me. I wish everyone could have parents like mine. They showed me what it means to love unconditionally, to give generously without expectation of anything in return, and to treat every person and rise to every occasion with compassion, empathy, joy, and humor. Bill and Kathleen Sampson, you are my greatest mentors and soul mates in this crazy journey called life. Much of what is contained in these pages came from your hearts, traveling through me as the channel.

I met my now husband, Neal Thornhill, when I was twenty and he was only eighteen, at a fraternity party... really. The odds were against the possibility we would stay together and build the dream of a life we now live, twenty-seven years later. He is truly my better half, in every way. I aspire to be more like him, I go to him for advice on every issue I struggle with, and I am awash with gratitude every day that he puts up with me and makes me feel so loved and understood. This book would never, ever have been written without his support.

I pray that my sons Jake and Joey, now nineteen and fifteen, will forgive me for all the examples I pulled from their lives and our conversations to flesh out points I wanted to make in this book. But I couldn't help myself. My two boys have helped me grow more as a person and taught me more about communication and true love than all my other relationships combined, for my entire forty-seven years of life. Thank you, Jake and Joey. You are my greatest loves and always, always will be.

Many beloved friends, family members, and colleagues have read this book entirely, or sections of it and provided me with incredibly valuable feedback. I wish I could take time to gush about all the great conversations we had and helpful input they shared, but I fear that if I did, I'd need one hundred more pages. Please know that your support, kind words, constructive suggestions, and encouragement of my writing process is what kept me going: Corie Skolnick, Kathryn Sorrells, Shelly Hickman, Sarah Shabbar, Amanda Sander, Laura Ramsden Gideon, Olivia Schiffer, Noemi Marin, Wendy Yost, Natalie Spiewak, Deepti Shoemaker, Lloyd Frank, Jennifer Strohl, Alisa Caron, Sharon Mazmanian, Jessica Angulo, and Julianna Kirschner.

I want to highlight four people whose assistance was especially significant. Chair of the Communication Studies department at California State University, Northridge, as well as my dear friend, Dr. Kathryn Sorrells, was generous enough to help me elevate the chapter on intercultural communication in ways I could never have done on my own. Sarah Shabbar has been many things in the few years I've known her, from student to teacher, colleague to friend, and so much more. She provided invaluable editing assistance, help with organizing the reading lists at the end, and insightful feedback from a millennial generation perspective, which was very important to me. Shelly Hickman is a fellow author whose work I am a huge fan of. Somehow we found each other and discovered so many uncanny similarities in our lives, our work, and our philosophies about almost everything. She read the book with her whole heart, engaging me in a conversation with her comments that allowed me to see my own book in new ways and as a result, to make important and necessary changes. Finally, there is Corie Skolnick. Corie is a gifted author, an unparalleled therapist (many, many people's lives have been transformed by her), and one of the most honest, wildly authentic people you could ever meet. Corie is the great mentor of my life. I would not be a writer if it weren't for her and I could write volumes to explain why that's true, but she knows why and that's all that matters.

A big thank you to my eagle-eyed proofreader. I read and listened to (vBookz PDF Voice Reader is the best editing tool ever!) this book over a hundred times myself because I was so afraid that an error might slip through. Still, Wendy Janes, proofreader extraordinaire, found quite a number of corrections that were much needed. I am truly grateful for her work on this book.

The cover design came together thanks to the combined creative talents of my father, Bill Sampson, and Kiran Robertson, who I've been lucky enough to collaborate with for years on my websites, promotional materials, and other design projects. She works the kind of magic that makes what I'm trying to say or show visually a million times better than whatever I started with. I am so grateful to you, Kiran!

Chapter five, which is my very personal description of the True Colors® personality model, caused me some anxiety as I was writing it. This was not because I didn't like how it was turning out... the opposite is true. I was so excited about using True Colors®, which I am certified in, to help my readers understand how to adapt to different personality types. My concern stemmed from the fact that I knew I'd have to request approval from the True Colors® organization to let me use their name and my explanation of their system in this book. I want to thank

Mike Jordan, for always supporting me in all my efforts to bring True Colors® to my clients and for connecting me with Cheryl Colette, who granted the permission I so desperately needed. And Cheryl, I thank you for not only saying "yes," but also for enthusiastically sharing how much you loved the chapter. As a fellow blue (explained in chapter five), you know how much that meant to me.

One final shout out goes to Angelica Valiton, a favorite former student whose photography skills take my breath away. She has the rare ability to capture the true essence of a person's inner and outer beauty in a photograph — maybe because she's blessed with an abundance of both herself. Thank you for making me giggle and feel like a supermodel during our fun photo shoot in my backyard, Angelica.

If I missed anyone, I am so, so sorry! Please let me know and I will be sure to include and mention you in the next book. I'm already starting on it!

Works Cited and Recommended Reading

Works Cited

Books:

Achor, Shawn. *The Happiness Advantage: The Seven Principles of Positive Psychology That Fuel Success and Performance at Work.* New York: Crown Business, 2010.

Achor, Shawn. *Before Happiness: The 5 Hidden Keys to Achieving Success, Spreading Happiness, and Sustaining Positive Change.* New York: Crown Business, 2013.

Bacon, Terry. *Elements of Influence: The Art of Getting Others to Follow Your Lead.* New York: AMACOM, 2012.

Blanchard, Ken and Johnson, Spencer, M.D. *The One Minute Manager.* New York: William Morrow and Company, 1982.

Brown, Brené. *The Gifts of Imperfection: Let Go of Who You Think You're Supposed to Be and Embrace Who You Are.* Center City: Hazelden, 2010.

Canfield, Jack. *The Success Principles: How to Get From Where You Are to Where You Want to Be.* New York: HarperCollins, 2015.

Carnegie, Dale. *How to Win Friends and Influence People.* New York: Pocket Books, 1964.

Chapman, Gary. *The Five Love Languages: How to Express Heartfelt Commitment to Your Mate.* Chicago: Northfield Publishing, 1995.

Cohen, Allan R. and Bradford, David L. *Influencing Up.* Hoboken: John Wiley & Sons, 2012.

Gallo, Carmine. *Talk Like TED: The 9 Public-Speaking Secrets of the World's Top Minds.* New York: St. Martin's Press, 2015.

Gray, John. *Why Mars and Venus Collide: Improving Relationships by Understanding How Men and Women Cope Differently with Stress.* New York: HarperCollins, 2008.

Goleman, Daniel. *Emotional Intelligence: Why It Can Matter More Than IQ.* New York: Bantam Books, 1995.

Harris, Dan. *10% Happier: How I Tamed the Voice in My Head, Reduced Stress Without Losing My Edge, and Found Self-Help That Actually Works—A True Story.* New York: HarperCollins, 2014.

Katie, Byron. *Loving What Is: Four Questions That Can Change Your Life.* New York: Harmony Books, 2002.

Kondo, Marie. *The Life-Changing Magic of Tidying Up: The Japanese Art of Decluttering and Organizing.* Berkeley: Ten Speed Press, 2014.

Sorrells, Kathryn. *Intercultural Communication: Globalization and Social Justice.* Thousand Oaks: SAGE Publications, 2013.

Tolle, Eckhart. *A New Earth: Awakening to Your Life's Purpose.* New York: Penguin, 2008.

Tolle, Eckhart. *The Power of Now: A Guide to Spiritual Enlightenment.* California: New World Library, 1999.

Tsabary, Shefali. The Conscious Parent: Transforming Ourselves, Empowering Our Children. Vancouver: Namaste Publishing, 2010.

Audiobooks:

Dyer, Wayne. "Success Secrets." Wayne's Blog. Dr. WayneDyer.com 7 October 2014. Web. 7 June 2015.

Robbins, Tony. "The Time of Your Life—More Time for What Really Matters to You." TonyRobbins.com. Web. 7 June 2015.

Lectures:

Achor, Shawn. "The Happy Secret to Better Work." TED. May 2011.

Gilbert, Elizabeth. "Your Elusive Creative Genius." TED. February 2009.

Taylor, Jill Bolte. "My Stroke of Insight." TED. February 2008.

Tsabary, Shefali. "The Conscious Parent." TED. November 2012.

Scholarly Article/Research:

Kale, D. W. "Peace as an Ethic for Intercultural Communication," in Larry A. Samovar and Richard E. Porter, eds, *Intercultural Communication: A Reader*, 10th edn. Belmont, CA: Wadsworth/Thomson, 2003.

Internet Article:

Kinde, John. "10 Ways to Make Your Boss Laugh." Humor Power. WordPress.com 26 March 2006. Web. 7 June 2015.

Works Recommended by the Author

Books:

Albom, Mitch. *The Five People You Meet in Heaven*

Ban Breathnach, Sarah. *Simple Abundance: A Daybook of Comfort and Joy*

Beck, Martha. *Expecting Adam: A True Story of Birth, Rebirth, and Everyday Magic*

Beck, Martha. *Finding Your Own North Star: Claiming the Life You Were Meant to Live*

Berman, Laura, PhD. *The Book of Love: Every Couple's Guide to Emotional and Sexual Intimacy*

Bridges, William. *Managing Transitions: Making the Most of Change*

Brown, Brené. *Daring Greatly: How the Courage to Be Vulnerable Transforms the Way We Live, Love, Parent, and Lead*

Brown, Brené. Rising Strong: The Reckoning. The Rumble. The Revolution.

Cameron, Julia. *The Artist's Way: A Spiritual Path to Higher Creativity*

Canfield, Jack. *Dare to Win*

Carlson, Richard. *Don't Sweat the Small Stuff and It's All Small Stuff: Simple Ways to Keep the Little Things from Taking Over Your Life*

Carlson, Richard. *You Can Be Happy No Matter What: Five Principles for Keeping Life in Perspective*

Collins, James. *Good to Great: Why Some Companies Make the Leap and Others Don't*

De Angelis, Barbara. *Soul Shifts: Transformative Wisdom for Creating a Life of Authentic Awakening, Emotional Freedom, and Practical Spirituality*

Dyer, Wayne. *Change Your Thoughts, Change Your Life, Living the Wisdom of the Tao*

Dyer, Wayne. *Manifest Your Destiny: The Nine Spiritual Principles of Getting Everything You Want*

Dyer, Wayne. *The Secrets to Manifesting Your Destiny*

Elliott, William. *Tying Rocks to Clouds: Meetings and Conversations With Wise and Spiritual People*

Ephron, Nora. *I Feel Bad About My Neck: And Other Thoughts on Being a Woman*

Freston, Kathy. *Quantum Wellness: A Practical Guide to Health and Happiness*

Gibran, Kahlil. *The Prophet*

Gilbert, Daniel. *Stumbling on Happiness*

Gilbert, Elizabeth. *Big Magic: Creative Living Beyond Fear*

Gilbert, Elizabeth. *Committed: A Skeptic Makes Peace With Marriage*

Gilbert, Elizabeth. *Eat, Pray, Love: One Woman's Search for Everything Across Italy, India and Indonesia*

Gladwell, Malcolm. *Blink: The Power of Thinking Without Thinking*

Gladwell, Malcolm. *Outliers: The Story of Success*

Johnson, Spencer. *Who Moved My Cheese?: An A-Mazing Way to Deal with Change in Your Work and in Your Life*

Lamott, Anne. *Bird by Bird: Some Instructions on Writing and Life*

Lamott, Anne. Help, *Thanks, Wow: The Three Essential Prayers*

Lamott, Anne. *Operating Instructions: A Journal of My Son's First Year*

Lyubomirsky, Sonja. *The How of Happiness: A New Approach to Getting the Life You Want*

Meerman, David Scott. *The New Rules of Marketing and PR: How to Use News Releases, Blogs, Podcasting, Viral Marketing and Online Media to Reach Buyers Directly*

Muller, Wayne. *Sabbath: Finding Rest, Renewal, and Delight in Our Busy Lives*

Nepo, Mark. *The Book of Awakening: Having the Life You Want by Being Present to the Life You Have*

Northrup, Christiane. *The Wisdom of Menopause: Creating Physical and Emotional Health During the Change*

Northrup, Christiane. *Women's Bodies, Women's Wisdom: Creating Physical and Emotional Health and Healing by Christiane Northrup*

Northrup, Christiane. *Goddesses Never Age: The Secret Prescription for Radiance, Vitality, and Well-Being*

Pausch, Randy. *The Last Lecture*

Redfield, James. *The Celestine Prophecy*

Redfield, James. *The Tenth Insight: Holding the Vision*

Richardson, Cheryl. *Life Makeovers: 52 Practical and Inspiring Ways to Improve Your Life One Week at a Time*

Roth, Geneen. *Women, Food, and God: An Unexpected Path to Almost Everything*

Rubin, Gretchen. *The Happiness Project: Or, Why I Spent a Year Trying to Sing in the Morning, Clean My Closets, Fight Right, Read Aristotle, and Generally Have More Fun*

Ruiz, Don Miguel. *The Four Agreements: A Practical Guide to Personal Freedom*

Silver, Tosha. *Change Me Prayers: The Hidden Powers of Spiritual Surrender*

Singer, Michael. *The Untethered Soul: The Journey Beyond Yourself*

St. James, Elaine. *Simplify Your Life: 100 Ways to Slow Down and Enjoy the Things That Really Matter*

Tracy, Brian. *Eat That Frog!: 21 Ways to Stop Procrastinating and Get More Done in Less Time*

Tsing Loh, Sandra. *The Madwoman in the Volvo: My Year of Raging Hormones*

Weil, Andrew. *Spontaneous Happiness: A New Path to Emotional Well-Being*

Welch, Jack. *Winning*

Williamson, Marianne. *A Return to Love: Reflections on the Principles of A Course in Miracles*

Williamson, Marianne. *The Age of Miracles: Embracing the New Midlife*

Zukav, Gary. *The Seat of the Soul*

Films:

The Secret

What the Bleep Do We Know?

Audio Programs:

Dr. Andrew Weil's Guide to Optimum Health by Dr. Andrew Weil

Waking Up: Over 30 Perspectives on Spiritual Awakening — What Does It Really Mean? [Unabridged] [Audible Audio Edition] by Jack Kornfield, Eckhart Tolle, Sally Kempton, Reggie Ray, Sandra Ingerman

Made in the USA
Charleston, SC
16 July 2016